For Reference

Not to be taken from this room

Modern Collectible Dolls

IDENTIFICATION & VALUE GUIDE

VOLUME II

PATSY MOYER

COLLECTOR BOOKS
A Division of Schroeder Publishing Co., Inc.

The current values in this book should be used only as a guide. They are not intended to set prices, which vary from one section of the country to another. Auction prices as well as dealer prices vary greatly and are affected by condition as well as demand. Neither the Author nor the Publisher assumes responsibility for any losses that might be incurred as a result of consulting this guide.

Searching for a Publisher?

We are always looking for knowledgeable people considered to be experts within their fields. If you feel that there is a real need for a book on your collectible subject and have a large comprehensive collection, contact Collector Books.

On the Cover:

Left: *14" composition "Mary Hoyer" skater, mohair wig, sleep eyes, eye shadow, knitted/crocheted pink skating costume, $395.00. Courtesy Stephanie Prince.*

Center: *20" Madame Alexander "Cissy" dressed as 1923 Bride with 18K white gold diamond ring. Also an 8" Madame Alexander "Wendy Ann" and "Bill," a one-of-a-kind set created for the 1993 Disneyland Teddy Bear and Doll Classic, $5,000.00+. Courtesy Chris Law.*

Right: *15" Vinyl Ideal "Shirley Temple" pink nylon dress, sleep eyes, rosy cheek color, $225.00. Courtesy Sally McVey.*

Cover design: Beth Summers
Book design: Sherry Kraus

Printed in the U.S.A. by Image Graphics Inc., Paducah, KY

Additional copies of this book may be ordered from:

COLLECTOR BOOKS
P.O. Box 3009
Paducah, Kentucky 42002–3009

@ $19.95. Add $2.00 for postage and handling.

Contents

Dedication

Dedicated with love and affection to my children,
Rick Moyer, Marilyn Ramsey, and Rob Moyer

Credits

My special thanks to Shannon Jacobs and the following people
who helped me with photographs and more:

Alvis, Helen
Applegate, Vickie
Beling, Elaine
Blue, Brenda
Booth, Lilian
Boucher, Vivian
Bruehling, Kevin
Busch, Millie
Cann, Priscilla
Cermak, Dee
Clark, Cathie
Cramer, Martha
Cresenze, Barbara
Crume, Debbie
Culmer, Rosemarie
DeFeo, Barbara
Domroe, Diane "Dee"
Doring, Dorothy
Dunham, Susan
Eddy, Diane
Edmondston, Kathy
Elam, Gayle
Flabian, Frances
Forest, April
Fort, Elena
Fosnot, Anne
Friel, June
Gervais, Cherie
Gladden, Scott

Gonzales, Angie
Graf, Mary Evelyn
Graves, Diane
Hansen, Judene
Hash, Amanda
Henry, Georgia
Hill, Janet
Hollywood, Waltraud, J.
Holton, Linda
Honnaker, Eileen
Hunt, Imogene
Jackman, Jack
Jackson, Maxine
Jensen, Arlene & Don
Jesurui, Delores, L.
Johnson, Judy
Jones, Iva Mae
Kinkade, Sue
Kleindinst, Sylvia
Kolibaba, Sharon
Krawczyk, Nancy
Kunz, Catherine
Laurenouics, Nancy
Lauseng, Virginia
Law, Chris
Lunde, Louise, M.
Marthaller, Julie
Martin, Connielee
Mause, Rita

Maxwell, Anita
McCain, Candy
McMasters Doll
  Auctions
McVey, Sally
Meisinger, Marge
Merideth, Carolyn
Mertz, Martha
Mertz, Ursula
Miller, Virginia
Millhouse, Peggy
Mitchell, Bev
Mitchell, Janet
Montei, Peggy
Murphy, Veronica
Nance, Donna
Newberry, Faye
Nichols, Roberta
Osborn, Dorisanne
Pardee, Elaine
Pettygrove, Marian
Pilley, Fern
Pogue, Gwen
Prince, Stephanie
Putney, Aletha
Ramsey, Becki
Robertson, Sue
Robson, Suzi
Rose, Helen

Sanders, Jill
Santacruse, Janet
Saunders, Gloria
Schoonmaker, Pat
Schuda, Pat
Shroka, Edna
Sipler, Minnie
Smith, Joanna
Smith, Pat
Smith, Timothy
Stallings, Mary Lee
Stanton, Louise
Sturgess, Ellen
Sutton, Linda Lee
Sweeney, Martha
Swope, Mary Lee
Tanner, Harold
Trowbridge, Mary Lu
Vinton, Virginia
Viskocil, Peggy
Vitale, Kim
Welker, Margie
Whyel, Rosalie
  Museum of Doll Art
Wick, Faith
Wilkins, Sue
Williams, Louise
Winder, Toni
Woods, Glorya

Introduction

Perhaps "modern" is a misnomer for dolls over 70 years old. One reason for this, however, is that some doll companies that made dolls at the turn of the century are still operating and producing today. For this book, I am grouping as modern, dolls made of composition, cloth, rubber, hard plastic, porcelain, vinyl, wood, and some other materials, as opposed to dolls of bisque, wax, wood, and china that were made before World War I. There are no easy cutoff dates and some spill over from one category to the next. This book will give you examples of dolls to compare for identification.

Collectors who want to know more about the dolls they have or want to collect, need to learn as much as possible. One way to do this is to research and arm yourself with books and magazines that deal with the subject. Another way is to seek other informed collectors. Beginning collectors should list their dolls with the prices paid, the size, marks, material, and other pertinent facts, such as originality and condition. Collectors need to be able to identify their dolls and one way to do this is by material.

Experienced doll collectors refer to a doll by whatever material is used for making the doll's head. So a composition doll has a composition head but may have a cloth, composition, or wood body. A doll with a vinyl head and a hard plastic body is a vinyl doll. The head commands the order of reference to the doll in relation to materials used to produce it. A doll made entirely of vinyl is referred to as all-vinyl.

It is nice when exact measurements are given to describe the height of the doll.

To identify a doll with no packaging or box, first examine the back of the head, then the torso, and the rest of the body, the usual places manufacturers put their marks. Some dolls will only have a mold number or no mark at all. Nursing students are often given the task of writing a physical description of their patient starting at the top of their head down to the bottom of their feet. This is also a good way of describing a doll and its attire.

Collectors like to meet and speak with other collectors who share their interests. For this reason we have included a Collectors' Network section in the back of this book. There are many special interest groups focusing on one area of doll collecting. These are experienced collectors who will consult with others. It is considered proper form to send a SASE when contacting others if you wish to receive a reply. If you wish to be included in this area, please send your area of expertise and references.

In addition, a national organization, the United Federation of Doll Clubs has information for doll collectors who are seeking, or wish to form, a doll club. The goals of this nonprofit organization focus on education, research, preservation, and enjoyment of dolls. They also sponsor a Junior Membership for budding doll collectors. They will put you in contact with one of 16 regional directors who will be able to assess your needs and advise you if a doll club in your area is accepting members. You may write for more information to UFDC, 10920 North Ambassador Drive, Suite 130, Kansas City, MO 64153, or FAX 816 891-8360.

Beginning collectors will want to learn as much as possible about dolls before spending their money. It seems prudent to investigate thoroughly all avenues regarding an addition to one's collection before actually making a purchase.

Introduction

Novice collectors may wonder where to buy dolls. There are many different ways to find the doll of your dreams, including dealers or shops that will locate a particular doll for you. There are numerous focus groups that list special sales. Collector groups usually post doll shows and sales in their newsletters.

Auctions may also prove to be an aid in finding additions to your collection. Some offer absentee bidding which is most helpful if you do not live near. Some also offer phone bidding if you want to be in on the actual bidding. Auction houses usually send out catalogs and are most helpful in answering questions over the phone or FAX. See Collectors' Network at the back of this book for more information.

All of the more usual sources may pale in comparison with the mushrooming effect of the Internet. Type in "dolls" in one of the search engines and you will get hundreds of thousands of responses. Trying to navigate the "Net" and finding what you are looking for is a daunting task made easier by some of our sources. And with auctions, like ebay which specialize in dolls, as well as many other collectibles, it can easily overwhelm the budding collector. You will need research to quickly know the attributes of desirable dolls so you can make decisions on whether to buy.

Not only are books, magazines, and videos available for collectors, but simply going to museums, doll shows, and displays is a wonderful way for the collector to see dolls. To help the novice collector, simple tips on what to look for in dolls are included in this book.

Just as the most valuable quality in real estate is location, location, location; a doll collector should consider condition, condition, condition. Dolls with good color, original clothing, tags, brochures, and boxes will always be desirable. The trick is to find those dolls that also have rarity, beauty, or some other unique quality that makes them appealing to the collector. It could be that only a few were made. It could be that a collector recalls his/her childhood dolls. Or it could be that a doll's manufacture, presentation, or identity make a historical statement. Other factors can also contribute to the desirability and popularity of a doll. Cleanliness, good color, and good condition are always desirable qualities.

An easy way to keep track of the money spent on doll collections is to utilize a money program on your computer, using a number and description to keep track of your doll, then entering the amount you spent. If you sell the doll or dispose of it, the doll can be checked during the reconciling procedure and will not be seen on your current inventory. This is just a very simple way to help you with your doll inventory.

This book does not mean to set prices and should only be used as one of many tools to guide the collector. It is the collector's decision alone on which doll to purchase. It is the responsibility of the collector alone to choose his own area of collecting and how to pursue it. This book is meant to help you enjoy and learn about dolls of our past and present and give indications of future trends. If you wish to see other categories or wish to share your collection, please write to the address in Collectors' Network in the back of the book.

Happy collecting!

Advertising Dolls

Companies often use dolls as a means of advertising their products, either as a premium or in the form of a trademark of their company. This entrepreneurial spirit has given us some delightful examples. Not meant primarily as a collectible, but as a means to promote products or services, the advertising doll has been around since the late 1800s, and continues to be a viable form of advertising. Advertising dolls now can be made just for the collector — look at the Christmas ornaments that advertise Barbie, space adventurers, and the McDonald restaurant premiums in their Happy Meal boxes. All of these dolls or figurines that promote a product or service are called advertising dolls. Early companies that used dolls to promote their products were Amberg with "Vanta Baby," American Cereal Co. with "Cereta," American Character with the "Campbell Kids," Buster Brown Shoes with "Buster Brown," Ideal with "Cracker Jack Boy" and "ZuZu Kid," Kellogg's Company with a variety of characters, and many others.

What to look for:

Dolls can be of any material, but those mint-in-box or with original advertising will remain the most desirable. Cloth should have bright colors, no tears, little soil, and retain printed identifying marks. On dolls of other materials look for dolls with rosy cheeks, little wear, clean, and original, retaining original tags, labels, boxes, or brochures. Keep dates and purchasing information when you obtain current products. This information will add to the value of your collectibles.

Set of three cloth Kellogg's premium dolls, "Goldilocks and the Bears," 12–13" tall, originally sold for ten cents plus a box top. This set, the second set of this type issued, is missing Baby Bear. They were lithographed and came as a sheet of fabric that had to be sewn together, some wear. $75.00 each.
Courtesy Harold Tanner.

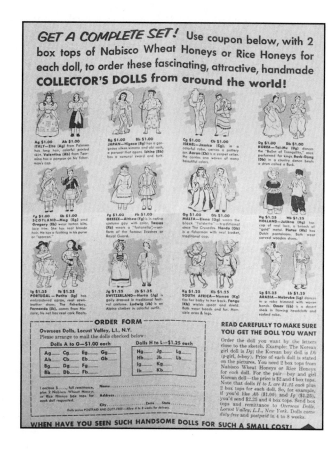

8½" hard plastic "Your Overseas Doll,"
sleep eyes, jointed arms, could be ordered for two box
tops from Nabisco cereal, $25.00. *Courtesy Elena Fort.*

Close-up showing brochure from "Your
Overseas Doll," offered dolls from Italy, Japan,
Israel, Korea, Scotland, Greece, Malta, Holland,
Portugal, Switzerland, South Africa, and Arabia.
Courtesy Elena Fort.

5½" hard plastic "Colgate Princess Doll," a Colgate toothpaste
and Fab soap premium, ca. 1951, with box, order form, and brochure,
all original, $15.00. *Courtesy Imogene Hunt.*

15" vinyl "Bell Doll" for Telephone Pioneers of America, rigid vinyl body, notice hard hat, original box, $75.00. *Courtesy Louise Williams.*

11" composition "Jolly Joan," waitress advertising Portland, Oregon, restaurant, ca. 1940 – 1941, by unknown maker, painted eyes, hair with painted blue bow, $125.00. *Courtesy Peggy Viskocil.*

15" vinyl "Gerber Talking Baby" by Toy Biz Inc., ca. 1994, $35.00. *Courtesy Virginia Miller.*

"Alice's Chess Set," a one-of-a-kind Madame Alexander creation designed by John
Puzewski, Daun Fallon, and Marianne Graf, includes 33 dolls from 8" to 21",
a quilted chess board, sold at the 1996 Disney World Bear and Doll Auction for
$42,000.00. *Courtesy Judene Hansen.*

Alexander Doll Company

The Alexander Doll Company made news on the financial pages as reorganization from their 1995 chapter 11 bankruptcy led new management to use the Japanese "kaizen" flow-type manufacturing. The company is owned by TBM Consulting Group and is located in the Harlem section of New York City. The new management has redesigned the production flow in the turn of the century Studebaker plant to allow groups of workers to oversee the manufacturing process from start to finish on selected items. Instead of one person doing one job all day, the group works together to finish dolls within their group, thus increasing productivity and cutting costs.

The financial and production changes seem not to have slowed the interest in Alexander dolls which have increased in popularity under the guidance of the Alexander Doll collector's club, a company-sponsored marketing tool that also has been used successfully by both Effanbee during the 1930s and more recently by Vogue with their Ginny club.

Beatrice and Rose Alexander began the Alexander Doll Co. in about 1912. They were known for doll costumes, and began using the "Madame Alexander" trademark in 1928. Beatrice A. Behrman became a legend in the doll world with her long reign as the head of the Alexander Doll Company. Alexander made cloth, composition, and wooden dolls, and after World War II they made the transition to hard plastic and then into vinyl.

The doll world was shocked these past few years with skyrocketing prices paid for some wonderful collectible Alexander dolls at auction including $56,000.00 for an 8" hard plastic doll re-dressed as the Infante of Prague. Alexander's rare and beautiful mint dolls continue to attract young collectors. Alexander dolls continue to increase in value as shown by one-of-a-kind fully documented special dolls as they appear on the market. These should continue to gain in value with the support of the avid Alexander fans.

One of the Alexander company's luckiest breaks came when they obtained the exclusive license to produce the Dionne Quintuplets dolls in 1934. The Alexander Dionne Quintuples were introduced in 1935, and were made in both cloth and composition, as babies and as toddlers. Some of the rarer groups are those in the bathtub set and sets with the wooden playground accessories like the carousel or Ferris wheel. Other companies tried to fill out their lines with matching sets of five identical dolls even though this brought copyright suits from Madame Alexander. Quintuplet collectors collect not only dolls, but clothing, photographs, and a large assortment of other related memorabilia.

Quint News is published quarterly by Jimmy and Fay Rodolfos, founders of a nonprofit group, Dionne Quint Collectors, PO Box 2527, Woburn MA 01888, at $10.00 a year.

For photos of Alexander and other quintuplets see Quintuplet section.

Alexander Doll Company

What to look for:

Alexander cloth dolls should be clean, all original, with bright colors. In newer Alexander dolls only mint, all original dolls with brochures, tags, boxes, and accessories bring top prices.

Composition Alexander dolls may have minute crazing, but must have good color, original clothes, labels, tags, and brochures to bring the highest prices. Buy dolls with severe cracking, peeling, or other damage *only* if they are all original or tagged.

Painted hard plastic are transitional dolls and may be mistaken for composition. Hard plastic dolls should have good color, tagged outfits, and be all original. The newer the doll, the closer to mint it should be.

21" "Glamour 'n Glitz," one-of-a-kind, designed by John Puzewski, circa 1996, MA Las Vegas Convention, $5,000.00.
Courtesy Judene Hansen.

21" "Eliza Doolittle," one-of-a-kind, designed by Daun Fallon, Doll/Teddy Expo, $2,200.00.
Courtesy Judene Hansen.

21" one-of-a-kind, "Sir Lancelot" and "Queen Guinevere," created by Daun Fallon and Therese Stadelmeir for the 1995 Disney Auction, $6,800.00.
Courtesy Judene Hansen.

14" vinyl "Little Mary Lennox Trunk Set," created by John Puzewski for the Let's Play Dolls Division, from the book, *The Secret Garden*, 1995 Disney World Bear and Doll Auction, $7,800.00.
Courtesy Judene Hansen.

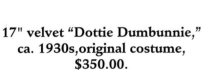

17" velvet "Dottie Dumbunnie," ca. 1930s, original costume, $350.00.
Courtesy Virginia Miller.

Alexander Doll Company

17" all-cloth "Scarecrow" character from movie
The Wizard of Oz, **ca. 1939, $500.00.**
Courtesy Martha Sweeney.

Left: 18" composition "Alice in Wonderland,"
unplayed with, original box, $775.00.

Right: 17" composition "Sonja Henie," one cloudy
eye, no crazing, good color, $1,250.00.
Courtesy McMasters Doll Auctions.

21½" composition "Bride," tagged dress,
mohair wig, orangdy princess style dress,
$535.00. *Courtesy Jill Sanders.*

18" composition "Wendy Ann," all original, human hair wig, sleep eyes, eye shadow, clover foil tag, $550.00.
Courtesy Stephanie Prince.

13" composition "Princess," blue tin sleep eyes, original tagged dress and hat, $300.00.
Courtesy Stephanie Prince.

18" composition doll in long bridesmaid-type formal, sleep eyes, eye shadow, $350.00. *Courtesy Sylvia Kleindinst.*

Alexander Doll Company

14" composition "Karen Ballerina," all original, marked Alexander on head, $595.00. *Courtesy Sally McVey.*

14" composition "Kate Greenway," all original, eyeshadow over glassene sleep eyes, $675.00.
Courtesy Sharon Kolibaba.

17" composition "Princess Elizabeth," blonde human hair wig, $1,000.00. *Courtesy Suzi Robson.*

14" composition "W.A.V.E.,"
ca. 1943, $700.00. *Courtesy Glorya Woods.*

15" composition "Jane Withers"
with script name pin, all original,
$1,000.00. *Courtesy Mary Evelyn Graf.*

Composition "Betty" in Girl Scout uniform,
$600.00.
Courtesy Dee Domroe.

Alexander Doll Company

10½" composition character, "Three Little Pigs," $400.00. *Courtesy Rita Mause.*

11" composition character, "Dopey," tagged clothes, cloth body, $650.00. *Courtesy Debbie Crume.*

Left: 11" composition "Butch," tagged outfit, $140.00.

Right: "Baby McGuffey," tagged outfit, $145.00.
Courtesy McMasters Doll Auctions.

8" hard plastic "Scarlett,"
$50.00. *Courtesy Vivian Boucher.*

17" hard plastic "Scarlett," $550.00.
Courtesy McMasters Doll Auctions.

15" vinyl "Sleeping Beauty," ca. 1959,
$300.00. *Private collection.*

Alexander Doll Company

17½" hard plastic "Alice in Wonderland"
(Maggie face), $365.00.
Courtesy Sally McVey.

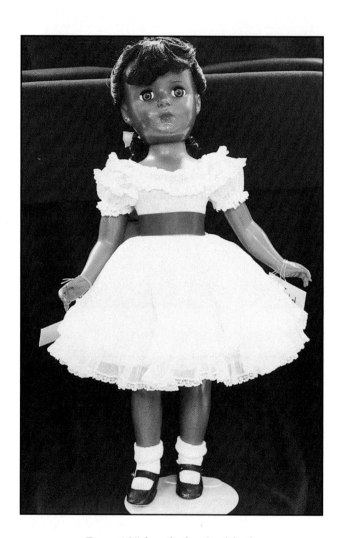

Rare 18" hard plastic, black
"Cynthia," all original in tagged outfit,
$875.00. *Courtesy Sally McVey.*

21" hard plastic "Piper Laurie,"
ca. 1950, $2,500.00.
Courtesy Debbie Crume.

14" hard plastic "Princess Margaret Rose,"
$250.00.
Courtesy Diane Eddy.

14" painted hard plastic "Nina Ballerina,"
$400.00.
Courtesy Sally McVey.

8" hard plastic "Wendy Ann,"
$35.00. *Private collection.*

Alexander Doll Company

14" hard plastic "McGuffy Ana," ca. 1948, hard-to-find pink corduroy coat and matching hat, pink organdy dress, $1,200.00. *Courtesy Sharon Kolibaba.*

20" hard plastic "Cissy," all original tagged dress, $350.00. *Courtesy Angie Gonzales.*

17" hard plastic "Maggie Mix-up," #1850, sleep eyes, freckles, vinyl arms, jointed ankles, pink capri pants, green satin heels, $325.00. *Courtesy Sally McVey.*

14" hard plastic "Jo," from *Little Women,*
$450.00. *Courtesy Angie Gonzales.*

29" vinyl "Alice in Wonderland," ca. 1952,
$700.00. *Courtesy Debbie Crume.*

20" hard plastic "Cissy," boxed,
in black formal with rose trim,
$675.00. *Courtesy McMasters Doll Auctions.*

Alexander Doll Company

14" vinyl "Easter Doll," hard plastic body, yellow dress and bonnet, ca. 1968, $225.00. *Courtesy McMasters Doll Auctions.*

17" vinyl "Madeline," #1854, ca. 1961, dark hair, tagged dress, all original, hard plastic body with jointed wrists, elbows, and knees, $425.00. *Courtesy Sally McVey.*

Louis Amberg & Sons

Louis Amberg and Sons were in business from about 1878 until 1930. They were located in Cincinnati, Ohio, prior to 1898, and in New York City after that. They used other names before 1907. Amberg imported dolls made by other firms. They were one of the first manufacturers to produce all American-made dolls in quantities. As early as 1911, they made cold press composition dolls with straw-stuffed bodies and composition lower arms. In 1915 they introduced a character doll, Charlie Chaplin, which was a big hit for them. In 1918 Otto Denivelle joined the firm and introduced a hot press baking process for making composition dolls. "Mibs," a soulful composition child with molded hair and painted eyes was introduced in 1921. The company was soon making Mama and "Baby Peggy" dolls. In 1927, they introduced the Vanta baby, which promoted Vanta baby clothing. In 1928 Amberg patented a waist joint and used several different heads on this torso, one of which was called the "It" doll. In 1930, Amberg was sold to Horsman who continued to make some of the more popular lines.

What to look for:

Amberg produced some very interesting composition characters and being able to recognize these early dolls will be a plus for you. Labeled clothing, good color, and minimal crazing are points to keep in mind when searching flea markets, estate sales, or garage sales for these dolls.

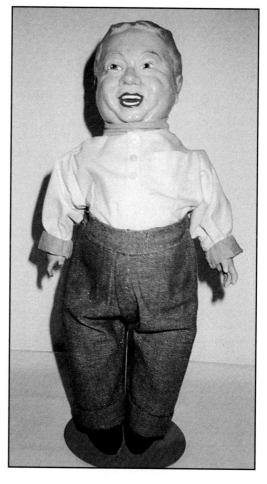

14" composition "John Bunny," ca. 1914, $450.00. John Bunny, 1863 – 1915, an actor, joined the Vitagraph Company in 1910 to make movies. Weighing 300 pounds or more, Bunny played a comic in silent movies. Made many comedy shorts in the next five years before he died. *Courtesy Mary Evelyn Graf.*

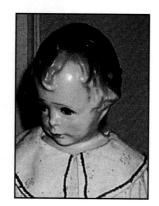

A very winsome 16" composition character doll named "Mibs" has a cloth label on her dress, ca. 1921, designed by Hazel Drukker, $700.00.
Courtesy Judy Johnson.

American Character

American Character Doll Co. (1919+, New York City) first made composition dolls. In 1923 they began using Petite as a tradename for mama and character dolls. They later made cloth, hard plastic, and vinyl dolls. American Character "Toni" dolls from the late 1950s are an interesting reflection of society's acceptance of women and girls focusing on primping and beauty, concentrating on hair. The "Which twin has the Toni" ad campaigns and dolls used to advertise Toni Permanent Waves were common to the era. Toni, Sweet Sue, Tressy, Mary Makeup, and other dolls with high heels and fashion-type figures all reflect the focus on women as objects of beauty that remains an ongoing theme in dolls.

What to look for:

Composition American Character dolls should have good color, little crazing, and tagged original outfits or appropriate copies of original costumes using natural or period fabrics.

Hard plastic and vinyl dolls should have great color, be clean, and should be dressed in original costumes with tags, labels, and brochures intact. Again, the newer the doll, the more complete and closer to mint it must be to command higher prices. Reject soiled or nude dolls unless they have wonderful color and you have original clothes you can use to redress them.

13" composition "Puggy," tagged outfit, painted features, frowning face, lacks hat, $500.00. *Courtesy Stephanie Prince.*

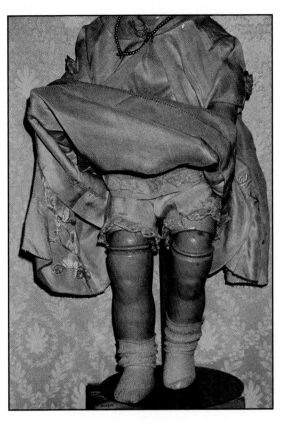

22" composition "America's Wonder Doll," ca. 1920s, $450.00.
Some early composition dolls may be found with ball-jointed
composition bodies like those used on antique dolls.
Courtesy Cherie Gervais.

14" composition "Sally," marked A.C.D.
Inc., molded and painted brown hair,
glassene sleep eyes, $175.00.
Courtesy Bev Mitchell.

18" hard plastic "Sweet Sue" walker, original outfit, $275.00.
Courtesy Peggy Viskocil.

24" vinyl "Sweet Sue," tagged,
all original, mint-in-box, $500.00.
Courtesy Barbara DeFeo.

18" hard plastic "Sweet Sue,"
with saran wig, in bridal gown with
cardboard trunk and wardrobe,
$500.00. *Courtesy Sally McVey.*

20" vinyl "Sweet Sue Sophisticate,"
a high-heeled adult, all original with box,
$375.00. *Courtesy Sally McVey.*

18" vinyl "Sweet Sue Sophisticate" in blue formal with
long cape/coat, hard plastic adult jointed body, painted
fingernails, **$400.00.** *Courtesy Barbara DeFeo.*

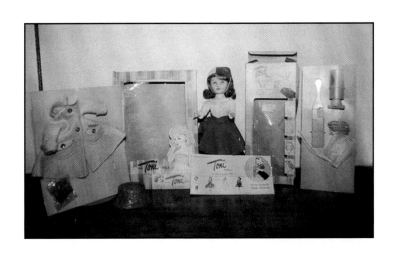

10½" vinyl "Toni"
with extra wardrobe, **$200.00+.**
Courtesy Cathie Clark.

Arranbee

Arranbee Doll Co. was located in New York from 1922 until 1958. It was sold to Vogue Doll Co. who used the molds until 1961. Some of their bisque dolls were made by Armand Marseille and Simon & Halbig. Made composition baby, child, and mama dolls. Early dolls have an eight-sided tag. They went on to make hard plastic and vinyl dolls, many using the R & B trademark. Some hard plastic and vinyl dolls (Littlest Angel and Li'l Imp) were made for Vogue by the Arranbee division and may be marked by either.

What to look for:

Composition dolls should have good color, only very fine crazing if any, and original clothes or appropriate copies. Always look for mint-in-box and tagged dolls in excellent to mint condition. Hard plastic and vinyl dolls should be clean with bright rosy cheek color, tagged or labeled clothes, preferably with brochures and/or boxes to command higher prices in the future.

7" composition "My Dream Babies,"
all original, mint-in box, $900.00+.
Made to compete with Alexander's
Dionne quintupletes. *Courtesy Georgia Henry.*

Arranbee composition marked dolls.
Left: 18" "Nancy," blue sleep eyes, closed mouth,
blonde mohair wig, $300.00. Right: 18" "Debu'-
teen," brown sleep eyes, auburn human hair wig,
$225.00. *Courtesy Veronica Murphy.*

12" composition "Nancy"
with marked cardboard trunk, $375.00.
Courtesy Lilian Booth.

"Nancy" was an all-composition child with bent
arms, and painted, molded hair, a competitor for
Effanbee's Patsy. 12" composition "Nancy"
variant, in trunk with wardrobe, $350.00.
Courtesy Lilian Booth.

Arranbee

12" composition "Nancy," all
original in wooden marked
trunk, with original wardrobe,
$400.00+.
Courtesy Lilian Booth.

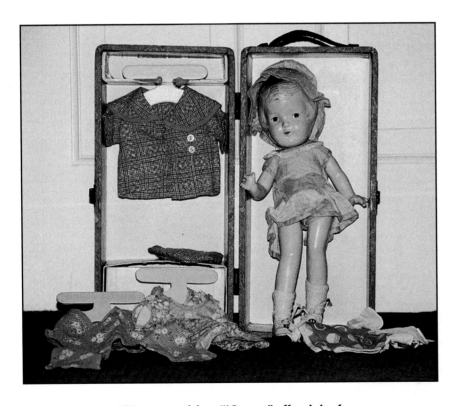

12" composition "Nancy," all original
with red wooden trunk and original wardrobe,
$300.00+. *Courtesy Lilian Booth.*

20" composition "Nancy" with
original wardrobe and trunk, $750.00.
Courtesy Cherie Gervais.

14" hard plastic "Nanette" in wardrobe trunk with 1955 catalog, $350.00.
Courtesy Sally McVey.

16" hard plastic "Nancy Lee," $150.00.
Courtesy McMasters Doll Auctions.

18" hard plastic "Nancy Lee," all original, $375.00.
Courtesy Sharon Kolibaba.

11½" vinyl "Littlest Angel," marked, in original #7 Birthday Dress, with brochure showing other costumes available, $50.00. *Courtesy Imogene Hunt.*

10½" vinyl "Littlest Angel" Brownie, $25.00. *Courtesy Stephanie Prince.*

Artisan Novelty Company

Artisan Novelty Co. (Gardena, CA, 1950+) made hard plastic Miss Gadabout, Raving Beauty, and other fashion-type dolls with smaller waists and a suggestion of breasts. They generally featured a "grown-up" wardrobe of evening dresses, bride's dresses, negligees, as well as day dresses, and skating costumes.

What to look for:

Try to find hard plastic dolls with good color, original tagged clothing, or boxed. Look for 1950s costumes that are clean and bright. Usually not marked but may have boxes or hangtags. Have been found as a beauty queen Raving Beauty and in sports costumes such as Miss Gadabout.

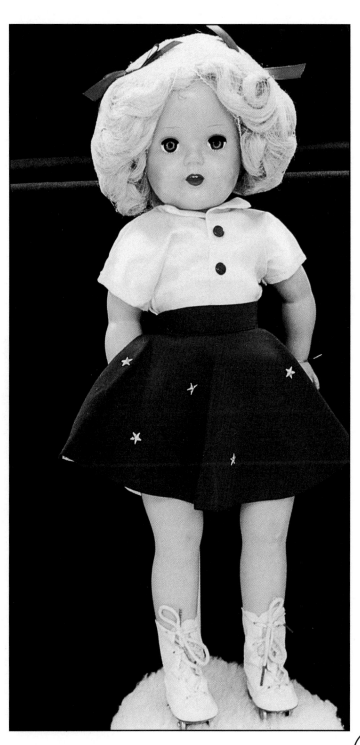

18" hard plastic "Miss Gadabout," original Michele CA outfit with roller skates, $295.00.
Courtesy Sally McVey.

Artist Dolls

These are original, one of a kind, limited edition, or limited production dolls of any medium (cloth, porcelain, wax, wood, vinyl, or other material) made for sale to the public. While a hot debate goes on in some doll-making and collecting circles as to the exact definition of an artist doll, we will use the above definition in this category. Some dolls appear to be works of art and some collectors may wish to have just that in their collection. Others define a doll as a play object and like to collect them for such. You, as a collector, are free to make your own decision to suit yourself. Still we can all appreciate the creativity which these talented artists exhibit.

What to look for:

One should remember that as with all collectibles, a well-made object of beauty will always be appealing. Some, not all, will increase in value. Study the dolls to find what you like. Some may only be popular fads.

A doll that is artistically done, in proper proportion stands a greater chance of increasing in value over time. You can enjoy it as part of your collection, rather than acquiring it entirely as an investment.

With artist dolls, one needs six examples or more of the artist's work to show the range of their talents. The artist doll category, however, does offer something for everyone.

6½" Sculpy girls by Elaine Pilsitz, $300.00+ each.
Courtesy Jill Sanders.

**Porcelain portrait bust by Linda Lee Sutton,
one-of-a-kind, contact artist for prices.**
Courtesy Linda Lee Sutton Originals.

**12½" porcelain "Tommara's Wash Day," limited edition
of 20, $650.00.** *Courtesy Linda Lee Sutton Originals.*

**17" porcelain "Goldilocks & Baby Bear — Let's
Dance" with 10" Baby Bear, limited edition of
25, $550.00.** *Courtesy Linda Lee Sutton Originals.*

**"Ivie's English Garden" wall decoration with original oil
painting by Lucy Braun, 17" porcelain "Ivie" by Linda
Lee Sutton, limited edition of 3, $1,950.00.**
Courtesy Linda Lee Sutton Originals. **37**

Artist Dolls

**21" porcelain "Kaiu & Polar Friends,"
limited edition of 10, $650.00.**
Courtesy Linda Lee Sutton Originals.

**21" porcelain "Tuesday," limited edition of 10,
$625.00.** *Courtesy Linda Lee Sutton Originals.*

**20" porcelain "Chen Ling & Pandora," with 7"
panda bear, limited edition of 20, $498.00.**
Courtesy Linda Lee Sutton Originals.

Sonja Hartman created this one-of-a-kind presentation shadow box with porcelain child holding dolls, 1996 Disney World Bear and Doll Auction, $7,800.00. *Courtesy Judene Hansen.*

4" pro-mat doll by Marcia Backstrom, $400.00. *Courtesy Jill Sanders.*

17" fimo one-of-a-kind "Christopher" and 9" "Pooh" created by Jane Bradbury from A.A. Milne's *The House of Pooh Corner*, Disney World Bear and Doll Auction, $5,600.00. *Courtesy Judene Hansen.*

5½" all-porcelain "Pippin" by Joanne Callender, #8 of 12, $550.00+. *Courtesy Jill Sanders.*

Artist Dolls

Porcelain Royal Family, ca. 1952 –
1960, by Martha Thompson.

Left to right:
20½" "Queen Elizabeth," $375.00;
21" "Prince Phillip," $200.00;
20" "Princess Margaret," $550.00;
12" "Princess Anne," $525.00;
10" "Princess Anne," $425.00;
10" "Prince Charles," $425.00.
Courtesy McMasters Doll Auctions.

18" porcelain Little Women
with stamped cloth bodies by
Martha Thompson,
"Jo," $325.00;
"Amy," $400.00;
"Meg," $300.00;
"Beth," $300.00.
Courtesy McMasters Doll Auctions.

20" porcelain "Lazy Sunday Afternoon"
created by Sonja Hartmann, 1995
Disney Auction, $5,200.00.
Courtesy Judene Hansen.

9" porcelain "Cousin Alice"
and 10" "Eleanor," ca. 1990,
by Kathy Redmond, $95.00.
Courtesy McMasters Doll Auctions.

6" porcelain by Sylvia Lyons, $325.00.
Courtesy Jill Sanders.

Porcelain Mary, the Madonna, with Baby Jesus
by Susan Dunham, no price available.
Courtesy Susan Dunham.

Artist Dolls

Cloth "Little Match Girl," made by Shirley A. Peck of American Beauty Dolls, souvenir of Region 1 Conference in Eugene, Oregon, $175.00, extra outfit, $50.00.
Courtesy Becki Ramsey.

Various sizes, hand-painted cloth dolls by Barbara Buysse; prices vary according to size, on resale: $300.00 – $1,200.00. Also: cloth "Topsy-Turvy" doll by unknown artist, ca. 1960s, $75.00.
Courtesy Barbara DeFeo.

9½" "Native girl," wax figure by Vargas, $350.00. *Courtesy Jack Jackman.*

10½" wax Vargas figure, "Charcoal Vendor," $300.00. *Courtesy Jack Jackman.*

18" china "Grape Lady" by Emma Clear,
$250.00. *Courtesy Helen Rose.*

Latex "Angela Appleseed" as child
and adult by Dewees Cochran.
12" child, $1,500.00; 17" adult, $775.00.
Courtesy McMasters Doll Auctions.

25" wax "Cuban" by
Louis Sorenson, $600.00.
Courtesy Cherie Gervais.

Artist Dolls

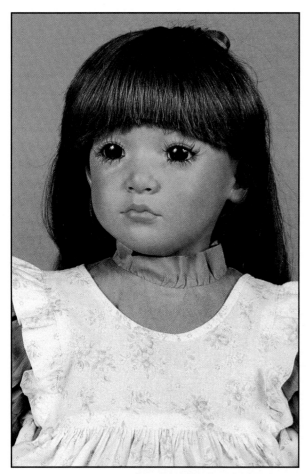

26" vinyl "Neblina" by Annette Himstedt, mint-in-box with certificate, $525.00. *Courtesy McMasters Doll Auctions.*

21" porcelain "Ballerina" by Suzanne Gibson, $125.00.
Courtesy Sharon Kolibaba.

22" wax "Uncle Sam" by Louis Sorenson, with cloth tag on outfit, $600.00. *Courtesy Cherie Gervais*

**19" all wood "Josephine," hand carved
by Sherman Smith, $1,000.00.**
Courtesy Sharon Kolibaba.

**6" wooden man by
Sherman Smith,
$125.00.**
Courtesy Martha Cramer.

**6¾" china with wooden body
by Sherman Smith, $250.00.**
Courtesy Martha Cramer.

**5¾" pink-tone china with body by Sher-
man Smith. If old china: $225.00; if
reproduction china: $100.00.**
Courtesy Martha Cramer.

Artist Dolls

5½" wooden doll marked "BIGSISTER,"
$25.00. *Courtesy Martha Cramer.*

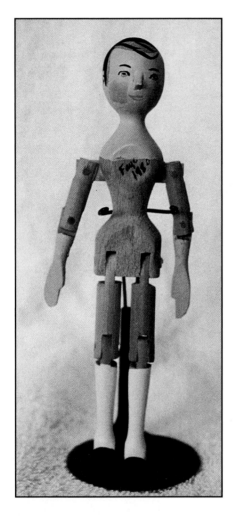

4½" wooden doll marked "BIGSISTER,"
$25.00. *Courtesy Martha Cramer.*

4½" wooden doll marked "BIGSISTER,"
ca. 1980, $25.00.
Courtesy Martha Cramer.

5¾" wooden jointed doll by Sherman Smith, 1968 special order from artist, $250.00.
Courtesy Martha Cramer.

5⅝" wooden jointed dolls by Richard Showalter, black, marked "RAS 87" $125.00; white marked "RAS 85," $75.00.
Courtesy Martha Cramer.

4" wooden English jointed doll by Eric Horne, marked, $75.00.
Courtesy Martha Cramer.

3⅞" wooden, strung with elastic, marked on foot "Czechoslovakia," pre-WWII, $25.00 each.
Courtesy Martha Cramer.

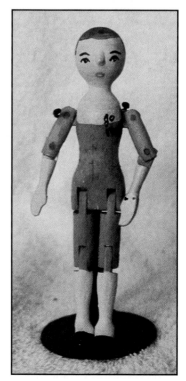

4½" wooden jointed, marked "BIGSISTER," ca. 1980, $25.00.
Courtesy Martha Cramer.

Georgene Averill

Georgene Averill (ca 1915+, New York City) made composition and cloth dolls operating as Madame Georgene Dolls, Averill Mfg. Co., Georgene Novelties, and Madame Hendren. Her first line included dressed felt dolls. She also made Lyf-Lyk and the Wonder line, and patented the Mama doll in 1918. She designed dolls for Borgfeldt, including Bonnie Babe. Her Peaches was a Patsy-type doll. A very talented designer and maker, she made wonderful cloth and composition dolls. The family had ties to Arranbee, as some in-laws worked in production at that firm. Averill's line of whistling dolls with bellows in the cloth body were clever and made to portray different occupations or ethnic backgrounds.

What to look for:

Georgene dolls of cloth, composition, or early plastic type materials. Georgene Averill was known for her felt costumes, and composition mama dolls with swing legs and criers. Search for bright and clean cloth dolls and labeled or tagged costumes on composition dolls with rosy cheeks and little crazing.

12" composition "Whistling Mah Jong," ca. 1924, in tagged outfit with long, black braid, $500.00. *Courtesy Pat Schoonmaker.*

26" rubber baby with cloth body in all original pink terry romper and bonnet, ca. 1945, $160.00. *Courtesy Janet Hill.*

Barbie

Mattel began making Barbie in 1959 in Hawthorne, CA. As we near the end of the century she remains a top collectible as children have grown up and become avid collectors of their childhood dolls. Of interest to collectors, too, are the fashion trends reflected by Barbie doll's seemingly endless wardrobe.

Marks:
1959 – 62: BARBIE TM/PATS. PEND.// © MCMLVIII//by//Mattel, Inc.
1963 – 68: Midge TM © 1962//BARBIE ® / © 1958//BY//Mattel, Inc.
1964 – 66: © 1958//Mattel, Inc. //U.S. Patented//U.S. Pat. Pend.
1966 – 69: © 1966//Mattel, Inc.//U.S. Patented//U.S. Pat. Pend//Made in Japan

Description of the first five Barbie dolls:
Number One Barbie, 1959
11½" solid heavy vinyl body, faded white skin color, white irises, pointed eyebrows, soft ponytail, brunette or blonde only, black and white striped bathing suit, holes with metal cylinders in balls of feet to fit round-pronged stand, gold hoop earrings.

Number Two Barbie doll, 1959 – 1960
11½" solid heavy vinyl body, faded white skin color, white irises, pointed eyebrows, no holes in feet, some with pearl earrings, soft ponytail, brunette or blonde only.

Number Three Barbie doll, 1960
11½" solid heavy vinyl body, some fading in skin color, blue irises, curved eyebrows, no holes in feet, soft ponytail, brunette or blonde only.

Number Four Barbie doll, 1960
11½", same as #3, but solid body of skin-toned vinyl, soft ponytail, brunette or blonde only.

Number Five Barbie doll, 1961
11½", vinyl head, now less heavy, has hard plastic hollow body, firmer texture saran ponytail, and now can be redhead, has arm tag.

What to look for:
Check those garage sales, flea markets, and estate sales for those first five Barbie dolls; even in played-with condition. Remember clean, undamaged, and original costumes should sound an alert. Barbie doll remains the number one collectible doll and has a huge following. Someone may be looking for those forgotten accessories and small items or body parts. It doesn't hurt to look in the attic at that old toy box, trunk, or carton that holds your forgotten toys from the sixties.

Barbie

Collection of eight 11½" vinyl one-of-a-kind Barbie dolls from the 1994 Anniversary Barbie Festival, $36,000.00.
Courtesy Judene Hansen.

The Irwin Airplane, 1964, has a turquoise body; orange instrument panel, nose cone, and lights; cream colored wings, interior, call numbers, and landing gear covers; chrome accessories; plastic window; rubber wheels. Very good condition with some discoloration of "chrome" and chips on nose cone, other chips and minor scratches, mint-in-box, $2,250.00.
Courtesy McMasters Doll Auctions.

Ken doll's 1963 Hot Rod with red roll bar, mint and complete $175.00 – 250.00; and Barbie doll's 1962 Austin Healy sports car, mint and complete, $160.00 – 200.00.
Photos courtesy McMasters Doll Auctions.

Above left and right: How do you tell all early Barbie dolls apart? The doll on the left is a Number One Barbie with pointed eyebrows and white irises. Four years ago she sold at auction for $4,100.00. The Barbie on the right has gently curved eyebrows, blue irises, and is a Number Three Barbie, if mint-in-box, $800.00+.
Courtesy McMcasters Doll Auctions.

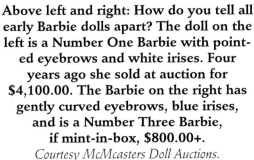

Fashion Queen Barbie, 1963, has painted brunette hair with blue headband, pink lips, original gold/white one-piece swimsuit, matching hat, plastic wig stand, and three wigs, near mint, $150.00.
Courtesy McMasters Doll Auctions.

Betsy McCall

Betsy McCall was a paper doll carried in *McCall's* magazine for many years. In about 1952 – 53, Ideal had Bernard Lipfert design a doll after the paper doll. This 14" Betsy McCall doll had a vinyl head, used a P marked Toni body, and had a glued-on saran wig. She was marked "McCall Corp." on the head, and "Ideal Doll//P-90" on her back. She came with a McCall pattern for making an apron. In about 1958, American Character made an 8" hard plastic Betsy McCall, and circa 1959, a 35" Betsy McCall with vinyl head and limbs and a plastic body.

What to look for:

Old *McCall's* magazines in the garage, attic, or basement with intact Betsy McCall paper dolls. Dolls should be clean with all body parts intact. These and the clothing to go with them can still be found.

4" porcelain figurines, ca. 1984, designed after original paper dolls. Left to right: "Back to School," "Introducing Betsy McCall," "Gives a Doll Tea Party," and "Most Christmasy Christmas," $15.00 each.
Courtesy Imogene Hunt, Louise Stanton, April Forrest, and Kathy Edmonston.

8" hard plastic American Character "Betsy McCall" in rain slicker and black boots, ca. 1958, $135.00.
Courtesy Peggy Viskocil.

8" American Character "Betsy McCall Skater," ca. 1958, replaced skates, $135.00.
Courtesy Peggy Viskocil.

8" hard plastic American Character "Betsy McCall Bride," circa 1958, $150.00.
Courtesy Peggy Viskocil.

Black Dolls

This category of dolls can be made of many materials, including bisque, ceramic, porcelain, china, composition, rubber, hard plastic, papier mache, vinyl, wood, wax and others. They can be made by a known maker such as Jumeau, Ideal, or Averill or they can be one-of-a-kind hand-crafted or modern artist dolls. Since less of these dolls were made, they almost always command higher prices.

What to look for:

Cloth dolls should be clean with bright colors; composition dolls should have minimal crazing, with original costumes or appropriately dressed. Collectors who like black dolls usually also like black ephemera and accessories. These can still be found in antique malls, flea markets, and estate sales. You may wish to find your own collecting niche here.

10½" French cloth seven-piece band, each with wooden instruments, 1940s – 1950s, molded cloth faces, black woolly hair, painted features, felt clothes, $1,000.00 set.
Courtesy Dee Domroe.

11" cloth Lulu Parsons "Mammy" in orange and black ruffled clown suit, blue and white check turban, ca. 1916, $500.00.
Courtesy Anne Fosnot.

11" velour Norah Wellings boy, painted features, re-dressed with original wrist tag, $250.00.
Courtesy Anne Fosnot.

17" cloth "Topsy-Turvy" with oil painted features, ca. 1900, $250.00.
Courtesy Dee Domroe.

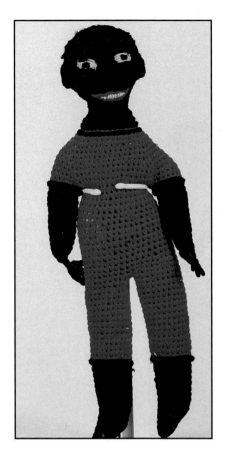

11" clay folk art "Mammy" with iron pot, washing clothes, unmarked, $200.00.
Courtesy Anne Fosnot.

16" crocheted boy with red one-piece suit, ca. 1920s, maker unknown, $100.00.
Courtesy Anne Fosnot.

11" cloth-over-wire Lulu Parsons "Nuthead Lady" in green and white dress with blue checked apron, holds cotton ball on head, $175.00.
Courtesy Anne Fosnot.

5" painted bisque "Nancy Ann Storybook" in long yellow striped dress, black mohair wig, $175.00. *Courtesy Anne Fosnot.*

5" painted bisque "Nancy Ann Storybook" with pigtails, plaid dress, and white molded boots, $150.00. *Courtesy Anne Fosnot.*

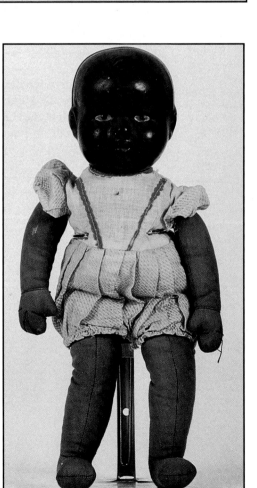

13" composition Allied Grand Doll Mfg. Co. "Jackie Robinson," ca. 1950, fully jointed with molded, painted hair and features, portrays first black baseball player in major leagues. $900.00.
Courtesy Rosalie Whyel Museum of Doll Art.

13" composition unmarked girl with painted eyes, open mouth, brown cloth body, original red and white romper suit, $250.00.
Courtesy Anne Fosnot.

9" bisque girl with glass eyes, mohair wig, crude five-piece composition body, marked, $250.00.
Courtesy Anne Fosnot.

14" composition E.I. Horsman boy with molded and painted features, cloth feet, compo hands, $250.00.
Courtesy Anne Fosnot.

King World Inc. "Buckwheat" from *The Little Rascals*, Hamilton Collection, ca. 1994, $85.00.
Courtesy Anne Fosnot.

King World Inc. "Stymie" from *Little Rascals*, Hamilton Collection, ca. 1994, $85.00.
Courtesy Anne Fosnot.

Cameo

Joseph L. Kallus's company operated from 1922 to 1930 in New York City and Port Allegheny, PA. They made composition dolls with segmented wooden or cloth bodies, as well as all-composition dolls.

What to look for:

Look for dolls with good color, little or no crazing, and original costumes — especially those that bear labels. Look closely at the sewing on clothing; the inside part may reveal whether it was done by a home seamstress or commercially made. Original clothing is always desirable; if it is intact you can use it on the doll — if not, you can use it for a pattern to re-create the style of costume your doll wore in the period she was made.

Avoid composition dolls with cracks, breaks, peeling, or lifting paint layers. Consider only if they have added attractions such as original clothing, labels, tags, boxes, or other accessories that may be salvaged for another doll.

Small size perfect 8" composition "Scootles" with molded hair, painted eyes, original blue sunsuit with hang tag, $875.00.
Courtesy Sue Kinkade.

Celebrity Dolls

Celebrity dolls are representations of famous or well-known real people, not literary or other fictitious characters. For example, Betty Boop and Charlie McCarthy were well-known personalities but were not real people. There are also many one-of-a-kind artist dolls of celebrities as well as those manufactured by various companies. Some of the more famous of the composition era were Shirley Temple and the Dionne Quintuplets. If you love the idea of collecting this category, be sure to read *The Encyclopedia of Celebrity Dolls,* by John Axe, which gives information on over 1,500 celebrity dolls.

What to look for:

Composition dolls should have good cheek color, but may have "blown" (dried out celluloid) eyes. It is hard to find a great composition Shirley Temple doll, but they are out there. As with all composition dolls, try to find a doll with minimal crazing, lifting, and peeling of paint. It might be acceptable on the body, but it is really detracting on the face. Original labeled clothing is desirable. Do not hesitate if it looks like it just came off the shelf; these are too few to last past the next customer.

Look for complete vinyl or hard plastic dolls in boxes or with brochures and hang tags or labels. One place to find these are the mark-down shelves of discount stores. Other places may be stores that focus on overrun or discontinued merchandise.

Celebrity dolls are made in every material imaginable. If that doll at the flea market or estate sale is vaguely familiar, it just might be a celebrity doll. You need to research this category well so you will be able to spot those dolls of interest to you.

11½" vinyl Goldberger "Dolly Parton," **$20.00.** *Courtesy Janet Santacruse.*

18" vinyl, talking Robert Englund as "Freddy Kreuger" from *Nightmare on Elm Street*, mint-in-box, $60.00.
Courtesy Faye Newberry.

13" rigid vinyl Jonathan Taylor Thomas as "Pinocchio," includes poster of the star, mint-in-box, $20.00.
Courtesy Angie Gonzales.

Vinyl Michael Keaton as "Beetlejuice," $60.00. *Courtesy Cathie Clark.*

9" vinyl Turner Co. Bob Denver as "Gilligan," with molded clothing, on vinyl base, $20.00.
Courtesy Kevin Bruehling.

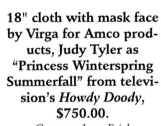

18" cloth with mask face by Virga for Amco products, Judy Tyler as "Princess Winterspring Summerfall" from television's *Howdy Doody*, $750.00.
Courtesy June Friel.

11½" vinyl Grace Kelly as seen in *The Swan*, mint-in-box, $40.00.
Courtesy Janet Santacruse.

10½" vinyl articulated Dan Haggerty as television character "Grizzly Adams," molded blond hair and beard, $20.00.
Courtesy Janet Santacruse.

Cloth

Cloth dolls are wonderful collectibles. Cloth dolls, originally children's playthings, are especially appealing for their soft cuddly quality. They are remembered nostalgically as their original owners grow into older collectors. A large number of makers and varieties are available, both as mass produced and homemade or artist dolls.

What to look for:

Sometimes a doll that is not entirely charming at first glance can reveal hidden attributes. For example the homemade cloth bride shown here was not so appealing with her simple embroidered features and applied nose and yarn hair. Looking under her wedding dress, creative underclothing was revealed including a corset, hose, and garter belt. Possibly made for a bridal shower, this is a very amusing bit of Americana.

Look for clean well-made dolls with bright, not faded colors in their costumes. Labeled or tagged costumes or always a plus. Check closely to see the sewing and the undergarments. Some of these one-of-a-kind or even mass-produced dolls can be utterly charming. Advertising, ethnic, and characters are especially collectible as they cross over collecting fields.

23" one-of-a-kind doll with meticulous undergarments including hose and garter belt, ca. 1920s, $50.00.
Courtesy Aletha Putney.

14" ethnic doll by Margas of Hungary, nursing mother with exposed breast and 3" cloth baby, $350.00. *Courtesy Martha Mertz.*

12½" felt Raynal Toddlers, ca. 1920s, original clothes except for shoes and boy's hat, $380.00 set.
Courtesy Connielee Martin.

The back of the Raynal Toddlers.

Cloth

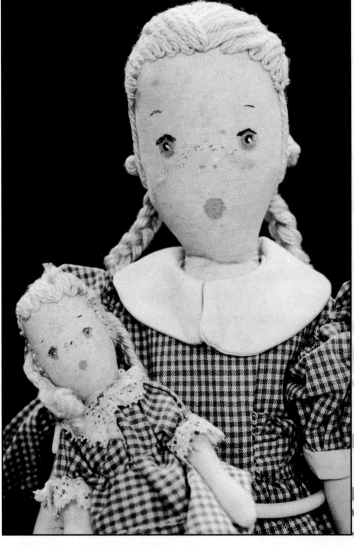

4" German post-WWII miniature nursery rhyme characters, "Goldilocks and the Three Bears," $100.00 set. *Courtesy Minnie Sipler.*

4" German post-WWII miniature nursery rhyme character, "Little Miss Muffet," $35.00. *Courtesy Minnie Sipler.*

14" doll with painted face, yellow cording braids, purple checked cotton dress, holds 4½" matching doll, $25.00. *Courtesy private collection.*

18" "Denny Dimwit," unmarked, cloth body,
jointed shoulders, flannel hands, three
stitched fingers and thumb, $195.00.
Courtesy McMasters Doll Auctions.

Molded mask face characters: 17",
"Popeye," mint, $250.00; 17" "Olive Oyl,"
$200.00; 14" "Swee'Pea," $250.00.
Courtesy McMasters Doll Auctions.

20" Georgene Averill "Uncle Wiggily,"
all original with hang tags, $550.00.
Courtesy McMasters Doll Auctions.

18" Ravac-type man and woman, soft sculptured stockinette face and body, painted features, wire armatures, $155.00.
Courtesy McMasters Doll Auctions.

14" Georgene Novelties child in Hawaiian clothing, hang tags, yarn hair, mint-in-box, $200.00.
Courtesy Barbara DeFeo.

20" German character, felt clothes, glass eyes, perhaps Fleishmann & Bloedel, $500.00. *Courtesy Dee Domroe.*

20" German character, felt clothes, glass eyes, perhaps Fleishmann & Bloedel, $500.00. *Courtesy Dee Domroe.*

20" German character, felt clothes, glass eyes, perhaps Fleishmann & Bloedel, $500.00. *Courtesy Dee Domroe.*

15" Lulu Parsons girl with human hair wig, button eyes, red dress with black trim, applied ears, ca. 1916 – 1920, $425.00. *Courtesy Anne Fosnot.*

17" "Topsy-Turvy," oil-painted features, ca. 1900, $250.00. *Courtesy Dee Domroe.*

15" Lulu Parsons girl with human hair wig, big round blue button eyes, sculpted nose, applied ears, ca. 1916 – 1920, $425.00. *Courtesy Anne Fosnot.*

Composition

Composition dolls have been made from 1890s and possibly earlier. Cold press composition describes the method of putting a mixture of ingredients (composition) into molds. The recipe for composition varied with each manufacturer, but at first glue was used to bind together such things as flour, shredded cardboard or paper, and rags. Later sawdust and wood pulp were used as manufacturers learned how to bake the composition in multiple molds in the hot press method. The mixture was more soupy when poured into molds than when pressed and the ingredients differed somewhat.

These doll heads were first described as indestructible as compared to the bisque and china heads that could be easily broken. The dolls were dipped in tinted glue baths to give a flesh tone and then later the features and coloring were air-brushed. Humidity made it difficult for the dolls to dry correctly in early production procedures, but later techniques were refined to reduce this problem. The big problem with composition dolls was their glycerin and glue base — when the surface became saturated with water, it would disintegrate. Extremes in heat and humidity cause bacteria to grow on the surface and destroy the painted finish.

Collectors need to keep composition dolls away from direct sunlight, avoid extremes in temperature, and keep a gauge in their cases to check the relative humidity. When the relative humidity exceeds 85%, bacteria have opportune conditions to grow and destroy the painted surfaces. Composition dolls should not be stored in plastic, but wrapped in cotton fabric that has been washed and well rinsed to remove any soap or conditioner.

Collectors who had this type of doll as a plaything in their childhood can, with a little caution, enjoy some of the wide variety of dolls still available. Included in this category are composition dolls by unknown makers or little known companies.

What to look for:

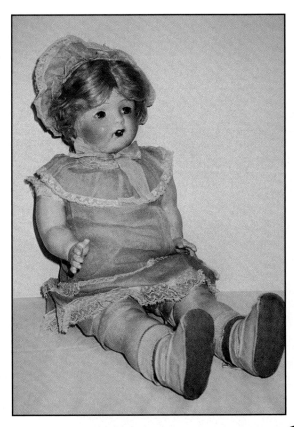

Great composition dolls should have no crazing, cracking, peeling, or lifting of paint. They should also have rosy cheek color and original wig and clothes. They may have blush on knees, hands, and arms. Added incentives would be tags, labels, brochures, or labeled boxes. Consider dolls with major flaws only if they have pluses like tagged original costumes, brochures, hang tags, or boxes, and they should be priced accordingly.

Unmarked 28" "Mama" doll, all original, mint condition, this type of doll would be a premium prize offered during the 1920s and 30s, $450.00. Mama dolls had cloth bodies with a crier and swing legs. *Courtesy Mary Evelyn Graf.*

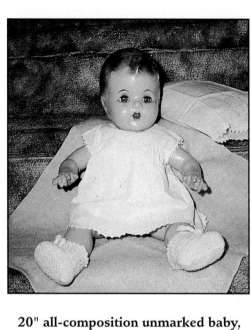

20" all-composition unmarked baby, molded hair, sleep eyes, open mouth with teeth, original silk dress and bonnet, and complete handmade layette, $350.00+. *Courtesy Sue Robertson.*

19" "Santa Claus," all original, ca. 1930s, $350.00. *Courtesy Becki Ramsey.*

21" unmarked all-composition child, red mohair wig, sleep eyes, re-dressed, ca. 1940, $175.00. *Courtesy Sue Robertson.*

Composition Patsy-type, $150.00 and Dionne-type nurses, $250.00. *Courtesy Georgia Henry.*

Composition

Old Cottage Toys dolls, 9½" "Pearly King and Queen," 7½" boy and girl, all in original felt clothing with sewn-on sequins, boxed with wrist tags, $265.00 for all. *Courtesy McMasters Doll Auctions.*

12" Fleischaker Novelty Co. "Beverly Doll," $325.00. *Courtesy Dee Cermak.*

8" Irwin Co. baby, ca. 1930s, with side-glancing eyes, $75.00. *Courtesy Connielee Martin.*

37" composition and papier mache doll, brown glass eyes, open mouth with painted teeth, cloth body, leather boots with red cloth legs, ca. 1920+, $400.00.
Private collection.

Unmarked 21" lady, unknown maker, $150.00.
Courtesy Bev Mitchell.

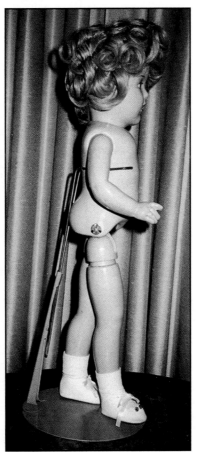

20" Shirley Temple-type with walker body, $500.00+.
Courtesy Dorothy Doring.

Composition

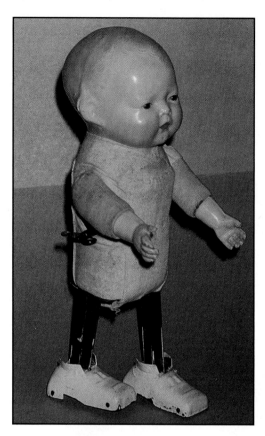

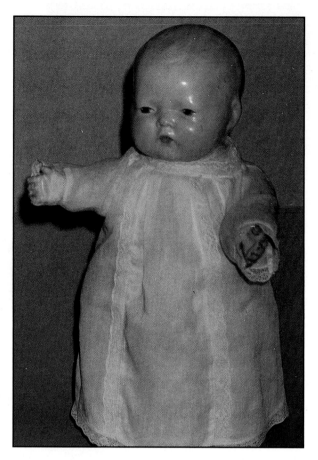

12" baby walker, marked "L.W. & Co.," possibly Louis Wolfe & Co., NY, with Waterbury Clock Co. keywind mechanism that lets baby walk, garments have finished opening for key, $400.00.
Courtesy Maxine Jackson.

Advertisement for Atlas Doll & Toy Co. rope jumper doll, from April 1928, *Toys and Novelties* trade publication.
Courtesy Patricia N. Schoonmaker.

13" Atlas doll, jumps rope as it is pushed, $400.00.
Courtesy Maxine Jackson.

Deluxe Reading

Deluxe Reading manufactured dolls from 1957 to 1965 that were sold at supermarkets as premiums — a reward for purchasing something else or groceries totaling a certain figure. They were marketed with several names: Deluxe Premium Corp., Deluxe Reading, Deluxe Topper, Deluxe Toy Creations, Topper Corp., and Topper Toys. They were of stuffed vinyl, jointed at the neck only, with sleep eyes and rooted hair. The dolls were inexpensively dressed, often as brides or in long formals. They also made 8" vinyl Penny Brite dolls with side-glancing eyes, and a vinyl carrying case.

What to look for:

Shown is a perfect example of a great doll to have in your collection. This Deluxe Reading cowgirl (page 74) has extra outfits, box, and instruction sheet. Look for dolls like this with good color, all original with box and accessories. They can be found priced quite reasonably at doll shows as collectors often pass by these for more well known dolls. Even out of the box, they can be charming additions to your collection.

8" vinyl "Penny Brite" with desk, $22.00. *Courtesy Gloria Saunders.*

Deluxe Reading

20" vinyl unmarked "Miss Fashion" doll, rigid plastic body, blue sleep eyes, rooted synthetic hair, with box, four complete outfits, and "how-to-dress" instructions, $125.00.
Courtesy Ursula Mertz.

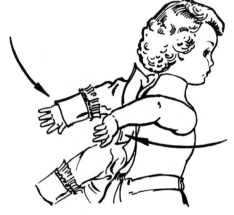

INSTRUCTIONS TO FACILITATE DRESSING AND UNDRESSING DOLL WHEN CHANGING TO COWGIRL BLOUSE OR SNOW JACKET.

1. Position both arms straight out behind doll as shown on illustration.

2. Slip on one sleeve.

3. Press arms together slightly, only enough to assist in putting on other sleeve.

4. Return arms to normal position and finish dressing doll.

23" "Little Red Riding Hood"
ca. 1955, tagged "all rubber" body, washable
synthetic hair, mint in box with book and
basket, $125.00. *Courtesy Sue Kinkade.*

Effanbee

Bernard Fleishaker and Hugo Baum formed a partnership, Fleischaker and Baum, in 1910 in New York City that would eventually be known as Effanbee. They began making rag and crude composition dolls, and even had Lenox make some bisque heads for them. They developed a very high quality composition doll with a high quality finish. This characterizes their dolls of the 1920s and 1930s and lasted until after the World War II, when the company was sold to Noma Electric. The company declined with the death of Hugo Baum in 1940, but had remarkable success with a series of dolls, including Bubbles, Grumpy, Lovums, Patsy, and Dy-Dee. Effanbee was a very entrepreneurial company during its prominent years using the talents of free-lance doll artist, Bernard Lipfert who created Bubbles, Patsy, and Dy-Dee as well as Shirley Temple for Ideal, the Dionne Quintuplets for Alexander, and Ginny for Vogue. Today, Effanbee Doll Company is owned by Stanley and Irene Wahlberg who have reintroduced many of Effanbee's 1930s favorites in vinyl, painted for a composition look.

What to look for:

Effanbee's early composition dolls are classics and the painted finish was the finest available in its day. Unfortunately, the finish on played-with dolls was prone to scuffs and bumps, not to mention that these playthings have to have been stored for 70 years or more and subject to varying degrees of heat, cold, and moisture. The biggest threat to composition dolls is changes in relative humidity. When the humidity is over 85 percent, conditions are ripe for the growth of bacteria that causes the paint to decompose, flake, or peel. Also avoid direct sunlight to minimize fading. It is necessary to keep composition dolls clean and in a stable environment avoiding high humidity. Composition dolls should be clean, with rosy cheeks, costumed in original or appropriate costumes. These were some of the greatest dolls of the composition era and a treasure when you find them.

Later hard plastic and vinyl dolls also have problems with cleanness and high relative humidity. You can, however, still find all original dolls with labeled or tagged costumes and good color and condition.

Group of five composition "Bubbles," ranging in size from 13" to 24", some in original costume, some re-dressed, with composition shoulder plate, cloth body, toddler compo legs, or cloth baby legs, finger points to mouth, designed by Bernard Lipfert, ca. 1924+, 13" 275.00, 16" $300.00, 22" $350.00, 24" $475.00. *Courtesy Becki Ramsey.*

22" composition with shoulder plate marked "Effanbee," cloth body, original costume, including teddy and full slip, $350.00.
Courtesy Donna Nance.

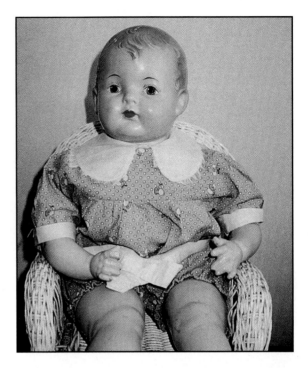

20" composition "Sugar Baby," painted features, molded painted hair, a mama doll with cloth body, crier, swing legs, nicely dressed, $275.00.
Courtesy Peggy Viskocil.

20" bisque doll made by the Lenox company, head marked "Effanbee//Lenox," an early attempt by an American company to perhaps compensate for World War I shortages of bisque dolls, only made for a short time, $1,200.00.
Courtesy Judy Johnson.

15" composition "Baby Dainty," cloth body, composition legs, original dress, $325.00.
Courtesy Pat Schuda.

Effanbee

18" composition "Lovums" with bent composition leg, all original in pink flocked dress, metal chain bracelet, box, $350.00. *Courtesy Marilyn Ramsey.*

Composition "Lovums," painted molded hair, open mouth, teeth, $300.00. *Courtesy Catherine Kunz.*

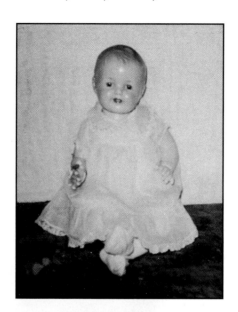

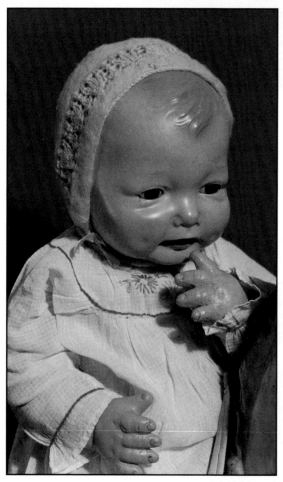

24" composition "Bubbles," re-dressed, open mouth, painted molded hair, composition shoulder plate, cloth body with bent cloth baby legs, $475.00. *Courtesy Becki Ramsey.*

Early 15" composition boy, with cork stuffed body, molded hair, painted eyes, composition hands, re-dressed, $175.00. *Courtesy Chad Moyer.*

Effanbee

15" composition "Grumpy," cloth body, swing leg, all original with cotton print and tan felt costume, Effanbee metal heart pinback button, $375.00.
Courtesy Marilyn Ramsey.

13" "Grumpykins," Pennsylvania Dutch Dolls, ca. 1936, dressed by Marie Polack as Amish couple, $500.00 for pair. *Courtesy Marilyn Ramsey.*

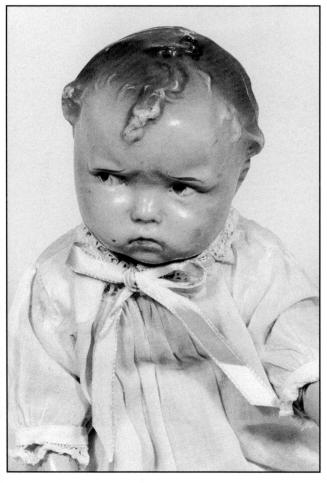

11" "Grumpy," mold 174, heavily molded hair, side-glancing intaglio eyes, cork stuffed cloth body, bent baby legs, composition gauntlet hands, tagged F.A.O. Schwarz outfit, $325.00.
Courtesy Marilyn Ramsey.

79

Effanbee's Heartbeat Dolls

Composition 16" "America's Heartbeat" doll complete in her original box, only the black tubing on the stethoscope has been replaced, and missing one sock. She has a windup box in her side, which when wound, gives her a "heartbeat," $600.00+.
Courtesy Mary Lu Trowbridge.

A Note About Your HEARTBEAT DOLL

My Dear:-
You know it took me a very long time to make such a wonderful playmate as your new Heartbeat Doll. But I truly feel that it was worth every bit of effort.

Because now you have such a wonderful and beautiful Baby ...a baby with a heart that beats just like yours! Isn't that exciting news? Don't you agree with me that you can have de—

lightful days playing with such an almost human baby doll? And there are a great many things to do in giving your Heartbeat Baby Doll loving care...many heart-warming ways to show her just how much you love her. I'm sure that you'll spend many fun-filled hours as the proud mother of such an adorable baby as your very own Heartbeat Doll.

your loving friend,
Aunt Patsy

Listen to Her Heart Beat...

A very important duty that you just *must* remember is to be sure that your doll's heart beats steadily. The stethoscope, which comes with every Heartbeat Doll, is made so that you can listen to her heart. Place the two ear pieces gently at your ears, hold the sound-box over your doll's heart and you'll be able to test her heart just as a doctor does. When you hear a weak beat it is time to give your doll attention. Then carefully and gently wind the key, located under her left arm. You'll hear a good steady heart-beat that will show that your doll is strong and healthy.

Give Your Heartbeat Doll Lots of Love

You know that love is ever so necessary to a baby. It's really as important as water and sun are to the flowers. With the loving care that you'll give your Heartbeat Doll, she'll soon become a very dear part of your life. Her daily companionship, and all the things you do together, will bring to you a feeling of mother-love that will make both you and your Baby Doll happy all the day through. And at bedtime you can croon a sweet lullaby that will send her off to Dreamland.

Make Sure Your Doll is Well Cared For

Of course you'll want to be a *good* mother to such a sweet baby as your Heartbeat Doll. Here are a few hints that will help you care for your baby just as tenderly as your own mother does for you . . . Keep your doll fresh and clean. See that you take her out for long walks in the fresh air and sunshine. Care for her clothes so that she always looks trim and neat — and tie her pretty bows properly. In *every* way be a good careful mother.

Your Heartbeat Doll Deserves a Party

Your playmates and friends will surely want to meet and know your Heartbeat Baby Doll. So it would be great fun to arrange a little party for her and invite your companions. Of course, your Heartbeat Doll should be the guest of honor and your little friends should bring their own dolls to make a very gay, happy party. You can then tell them all about your Heartbeat Doll. Just watch them as they listen to her wonderful heart that *really beats!*

How to be a Good Mother to your Heartbeat Doll

Effanbee

Composition "Sugar Pie" pair, ca. 1940s, also produced as Brother and Sister, Sweetie Pie, or Tousle-Tot. Sugar Pie boy is 16" tall, painted eyes, yarn hair indicates World War II material shortages at Effanbee, boy $350.00; girl $300.00. *Courtesy Janet Hill.*

Composition "Little Lady" in box, yarn hair, fur feather cape, embroidered inside cape, early 1940s, $600.00.
Courtesy Amanda Hash.

14" composition "Little Lady," gold paper hang tag as well as metal heart bracelet, original dress, unplayed with condition, light crazing, good color, small crack over eye, $175.00.
Courtesy McMasters Doll Auctions.

I WOULD like to tell you a little about the importance of hair styles for different occasions. For parties, for walking, for school or tea time—in fact for all the many things you and your Little Lady Doll will do—her hair should be nicely fixed.

You will certainly want to go to many places together and do many different things. I am sure your social life will be an interesting one.

Your Little Lady's hair can be combed, curled and styled in many different ways. The suggestions I offer you in this little booklet are only a few. You will soon be able to create many becoming hair styles that will bring out all the natural loveliness of your Little Lady Doll.

It may be very nice if you and your doll both have your hair styled exactly the same — then you'll be like Mother and Daughter—and that would be cute, wouldn't it? You will soon learn how to put up your own hair and keep it neat and stylish.

Aunt Patsy

A Stunning Evening Hair-Do

Dress Little Lady's hair with tiny ringlets on top, smooth down the hair in back. Roll the back hair upwards into curls and then if you wish tie on a snood. You will be delighted with the "Queenly" look that this hair style gives to your Little Lady Doll.

How To Use Your Little Lady Comb

The special Little Lady comb is designed to help you dress her hair easily and beautifully.

1 — Comb the hair to eliminate snarls.

2 — Take a small section and curl upward around comb.

3 — Hold the curl in place with your left hand, draw the comb out with your other hand and you will have a fine looking curl.

4 — Now that your curls are made, you can hold them in place with hairpins.

A Cute Style For Your Tea Party

Your dolly will be a hit at your tea party if you dress her hair as shown above. Comb her hair carefully and make two even rows of curls. A slight pompadour effect on top and a colorful ribbon bow completes this attractive tea-time hair style.

Little Lady Booklet, $25.00.
Courtesy Rosemary Culmer.
The yarn hair represented a World War II shortage of human hair wigs. Ever innovative, Effanbee provided a comb and instruction booklet with yarn wigs to show how the hair should be styled.

An Attractive Party Hair Dress

Comb your Little Lady's hair in an up-sweep style and make ringlets all around. Then tie a cute bow on top and you have a truly glamorous, stunning style for formal dances and for extra-special parties. This style is now the very height of fashion.

For Play Time

A pigtail and pompadour style is always very good. When you dress your Little Lady's hair this way she can romp, run and play as hard as you wish without having her hair blown about. And for school this style is very attractive. Braiding hair is very simple once you learn it.

Effanbee

20" and 24" composition "Sweetie Pie" dolls, caracul wigs, re-dressed, $300.00 – 350.00. *Private collection.*

Composition 20" "Sweetie Pie" with caracul wig, all original with paper heart hang tag, Effanbee heart labeled box, $425.00.
Courtesy Arlene and Don Jensen.

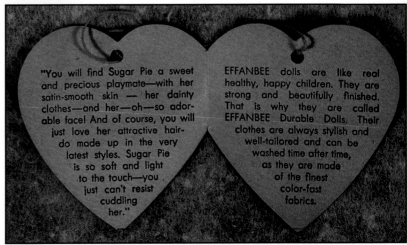

Effanbee's Historical Dolls

Effanbee put together the Historical Doll Series in 1939, advertising this as educational and historical. Three sets of 30 dolls, each 21" tall, costumed in silk, velvet, and brocade, were made and exhibited throughout the country. This was a very elaborate marketing ploy by Effanbee and has made these first three sets of 21" Historical Dolls very desirable.

Historical Replicas were 14" composition copies of the original sets, with painted eyes and only slightly less elaborate cotton costumes. They are very collectible as collectors vie to find all 30 examples for their collections. A very interesting collecting niche for those interested in costuming and history.

14" composition Historical Replica, 1939, marked "Effandbee//Anne Shirley," painted eyes, rosy cheeks, closed mouth, human hair wig, original outfit depicting costume of 1625, New York Settlement, $550.00. *Courtesy Bev Mitchell.*

14" composition Historical Replicas, "1658 – Carolina Settlement," and "1682 – Quaker Colony," $450.00 each.
Courtesy Sue Wilkins.

Effanbee

Two 14" composition 1939 Historical Replica dolls, "1872 – Economic Development," original dress, box, light crazing, $450.00; "1939 – Today" in lavender skirt, white blouse, light crazing, $460.00. *Courtesy McMasters Doll Auctions.*

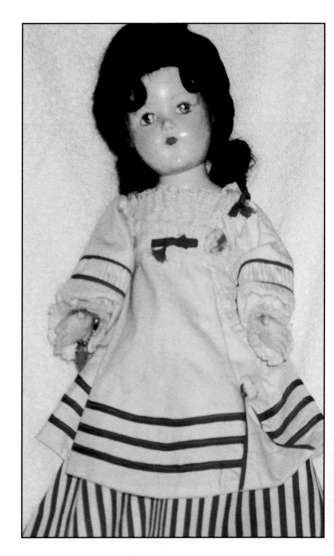

14" Historical Replica, "1816 – Monroe Doctrine," $425.00. *Courtesy Bev Mitchell.*

14" composition Historical Replicas, "1492 – Primitive Indian," boxed, $750.00; "1896 – Unity of Nations," light crazing, $325.00. *Courtesy McMasters Doll Auctions.*

14" composition Historical Replica dolls,
"1868 – Postwar Period," $400.00;
"1750 – The Development of Culture,"
boxed, light crazing, $430.00.
Courtesy McMasters Doll Auctions.

14" Historical Replica,
"1864 – Civil War," $550.00.
Courtesy Bev Mitchell.

14" Historical Replica,
"1873 – Industrial South," $550.00.
Courtesy Bev Mitchell.

Little Lady

Effanbee's Little Lady was an extension of the Anne Shirley mold, using the separated finger model designed by Dewees Cochran. Little Lady represented a glamorous grown up girl older than the toddler and little girl dolls on the market.

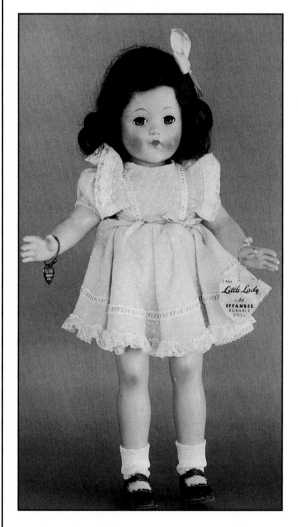

17½" composition "Little Lady," marked "Effanbee//USA" on back and head, human hair wig, with gold paper hang tag, $650.00.
Courtesy Mary Lu Trowbridge.

15" "Little Lady," in original negligee and undies, sleep eyes, human hair wig, gold metal bracelet reads "Effanbee Durable Dolls," circa 1940, $300.00.
Courtesy Marilyn Ramsey.

27" composition "Little Lady" with black human hair wig, black velvet dress with red rings on skirt and red ruffle trim, $625.00+.
Courtesy Vickie Applegate.

Similar to "Little Lady" was the 21" composition "Honey," human hair wig, sleep eyes, rosy cheeks, in original pilgrim costume, $425.00.
Courtesy Sally McVey.
This doll has fatter cheeks than Anne Shirley and was a transitional doll also made in hard plastic.

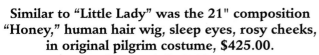

The Patsy Family

Another one of Effanbee's great success stories was the Patsy doll designed by Bernard Lipfert and advertised in 1928. She almost was not named Patsy. The same doll was advertised as Mimi late in 1927 and then as Patsy in 1928 in *Playthings* magazines. Patsy was one of the first dolls to have a wardrobe manufactured just for her. Accessories and clothing were sold not only by Effanbee but other manufacturers as well. She was made of all composition and her patent was hotly defended by Effanbee. What was actually patented was a neck joint that allowed the doll to pose and stand alone. She portrayed a 3-year-old girl with short bobbed red hair with a molded headband, painted side-glancing eyes, pouty mouth, and bent right arm. She wore simple classic dresses closed with a safety pin. She had a golden heart charm bracelet and/or a gold paper heart tag with her name.

Patsy was so popular she soon had several sisters, many variations, and even a boy friend, Skippy. Effanbee promoted Patsy sales with a newspaper *The Patsytown News* that went to a reported quarter million children. Effanbee also had an Aunt Patsy that toured the country promoting their dolls. In addition, they formed a Patsy Doll Club and gave free pinback membership buttons to children who wrote in or bought a Patsy doll. Effanbee tied their doll line to popular current events such as producing George and Martha Washington for the bicentennial of George's birth. They costumed a group of dolls like the White Horse Inn Operetta that toured the U.S. During the war years, they fashioned military uniforms for the Skippy dolls and also costumed dolls in ethnic dress (Dutch) or after characters in books like *Alice in Wonderland*.

The death of Hugo Baum in 1940 and the loss of income during the war years threw Effanbee into a decline. In 1946, Effanbee was sold to Noma Electric. They reissued a 1946 Patsy and later a new 17" Patsy Joan. Since that time the company changed hands several more times, until it was bought by Stanley and Irene Wahlberg, the present owners. Limited editions of Patsy Ann and Skippy were issued during the 1970s, Patsy reappeared in vinyl in the 1980s, and the Wahlbergs reissued Patsy Joan in 1995. In 1996 and 1997 they issued a new group of Patsy, Skippy, and Wee Patsy dolls in vinyl painted to look like the old composition ones. These are already becoming collectibles.

13½" "Patsy" introduced in 1928, commercial costume, painted eyes, molded headband, side-glancing tan/brown eyes with bent right arm, all composition five-piece body, $375.00.
Courtesy Becki Ramsey.

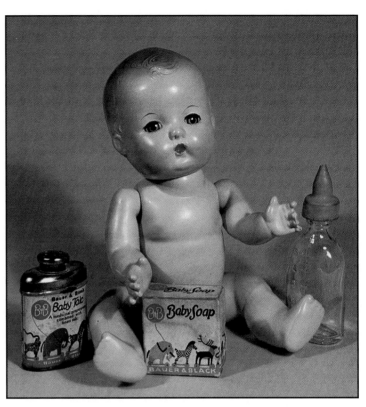

All original 11" composition "Patsy Baby" with sleep eyes, brown molded hair, cloth body, long organdy christening dress and bonnet, $375.00.
Courtesy Becki Ramsey.

9" composition "Patsy Babyette," nude, but with original labeled dress, $325.00; B&B baby talc and soap, $15.00; bottle, $15.00. *Courtesy Marilyn Ramsey.*

"Patsy Baby" all original in layette trunk with extra wardrobe, $600.00.
Courtesy Marilyn Ramsey.

Effanbee

Pair of 9" wigged composition "Patsy Babyette" twins in matching navy blue and white outfits, $500.00.
Courtesy Donna Nance.

**Left: 19" composition "Patsy Ann," 1929+, in tagged Mollye playsuit, $450.00;
Right: 14" "Patsy" in pattern made swimsuit, $400.00.** *Private collection.*

Two composition all original 9" "Babyette" twins in box labeled "Tousle Tot," both have golden heart paper hang tags, $750.00+.
Courtesy Pat Schuda.

Group of Patsy dolls, left to right, front row: two 9½"
"Patsyettes," $275.00 each; 14" "Patsy Jr.," $375.00;
back row: 14" "Patsy," $450.00; and 16" "Patsy Joan,"
$475.00; all in matching original or copy of original
outfits. *Courtesy Lilian Booth.*

9½" composition black "Patsyette,"
in original dress, $500.00.
Courtesy Pat Schuda.

13½" composition "Patsy" in white
felt coat and hat, copy of original
outfit, $425.00.
Courtesy Virginia Vinton.

9½" composition "Patsyette," in rare
"Alice in Wonderland" outfit and box, $500.00.
Courtesy Sharon Kolibaba.

93

Effanbee

Composition "Patsyette" in suitcase trunk, with extra outfits, $750.00+. Courtesy Mary Lee Stallings.

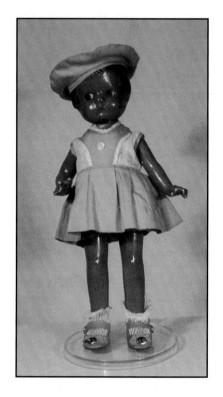

9½" composition mulatto "Patsyette," re-dressed in original Patsyette cotton outfit, some crazing, flakes on head, $450.00.
Photo: courtesy Scott Gladden.
Doll: courtesy Ellen Sturgess.

9½" "Patsyette," blue painted eyes, original dress and teddy, socks, and shoes, $300.00. Courtesy Stephanie Prince.

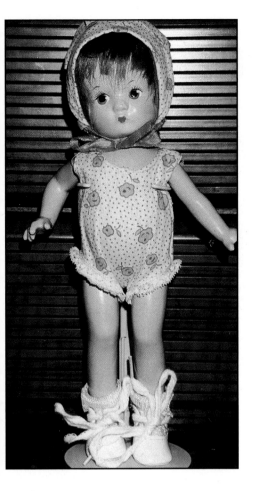

9½" "Patsyette," brown painted
eyes, wig, in original hat and teddy,
$300.00.
Courtesy Mary Lee Swope.

9½" "Patsyette" with red
wig and braids, in Movie
Anne Shirley costume from
1934 movie, *Anne of Green
Gables*, $275.00.
Courtesy Lilian Booth.
Effanbee dressed dolls in
their line to cash in on the
popularity of the movie,
and the costume changes
their identity.

9½" composition "Patsyette"
Dutch boy, all original, $400.00.
Courtesy Millie Busch.

9½" "Patsyette," all original in dress,
coat, hat, shoes, and socks, $300.00.
Courtesy Carolyn Merideth.

Effanbee

19" "Patsy Ann," circa 1933, human hair wig, original outfit, $525.00.
Courtesy Lilian Booth.

9½" composition "Patsyette" with trunk and wardrobe, including some original and some pattern made outfits, roller skates, and extra shoes, $600.00. *Courtesy Lilian Booth.*

Two 5¾" composition "Wee Patsys," marked "Effanbee," $350.00 each.
Courtesy Sue Wilkins.
Wee Patsy was advertised only as "Fairy Princess" with a marketing tie-in to the Colleen Moore dollhouse that was touring the country circa 1935.

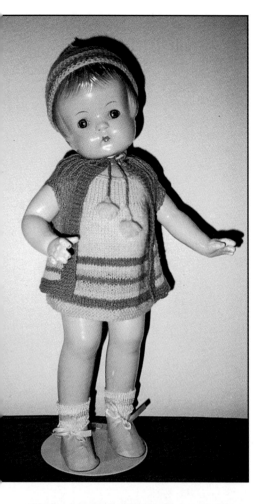

19" composition "Patsy Ann," original knitted sweater/dress and cap, note pink and blue striped socks, $475.00. *Courtesy Brenda Blue.*

Two 5¾" "Wee Patsy" dolls original castle dollhouse box on left, $525.00; with wardrobe suitcase on right, $650.00. *Courtesy Mary Lee Stallings.*

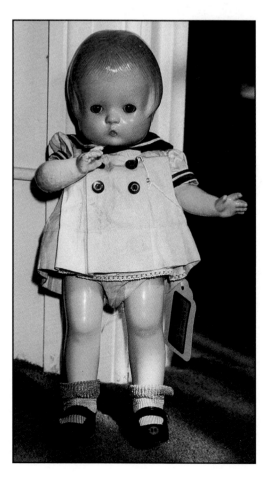

14" composition "Patsy" with sleep eyes, original dress, $475.00. *Courtesy Lilian Booth.*

9" composition "Patsy Mae" cloth body, old dress, $850.00; 27" "Patrica Ruth" with all composition body, $750.00.
Photo: courtesy Scott Gladden.
Doll: courtesy Ellen Sturgess.

Effanbee

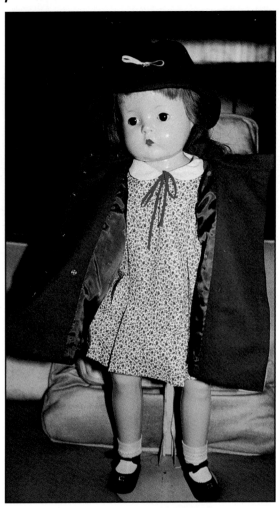

29" composition "Patsy Mae" re-dressed, $900.00. *Courtesy Pat Schuda.* She is really a mama doll with cloth body, swing legs, and crier.

14" composition sleep-eye "Patsy" in original red silk dress and hat, shoes, and bracelet, ca. 1932, $500.00. *Photo: courtesy Scott Gladden. Doll: courtesy Ellen Sturgess.*

22" composition "Patsy" mama doll with cloth body, crier, swing legs, original dress, teddy, wig, some crazing, $300.00. *Photo: courtesy Scott Gladden. Doll: courtesy Ellen Sturgess.*

14 composition "Anne Shirley" character from *Anne of Green Gables* 1934 movie, has her own paper heart hang tag stating "I am Anne Shirley" plus a heart sticker on her dress, $600.00 with box.
Courtesy McMasters Doll Auctions.

19" "Betty Bounce," tousle head, marked "Lovums" using a marked Patsy Ann body, wears wool coat with curly lamb trim, $350.00.
Courtesy Edna Shroka.

14" composition "Patsy" mama doll with cloth torso, compo arms and legs, marked "Patsy" in half circle on shoulder plate, open mouth, blonde wig, old clothes, $150.00.
Photo: courtesy Scott Gladden.
Doll: courtesy Ellen Sturgess.

16" composition "Mary Lee" variant using a marked Mary Lee head on a marked Patsy Joan body, $300.00.
Courtesy Pat Smith.

Effanbee

1996 F.A.O. Schwarz 13" vinyl "Patsy,"
$69.00. *Courtesy Lilian Booth.*

1996 17" vinyl "Patsy Joan" with wig
and heart bracelet, $85.00.
Courtesy Lilian Booth.

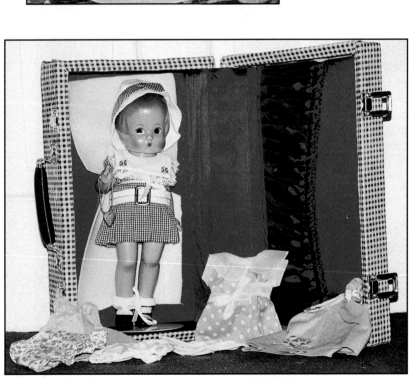

1996 vinyl "Patsy" in trunk
with wardrobe, $115.00.
Courtesy Lilian Booth.

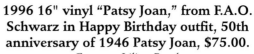

**1996 16" vinyl "Patsy Joan," from F.A.O.
Schwarz in Happy Birthday outfit, 50th
anniversary of 1946 Patsy Joan, $75.00.**
Courtesy Lilian Booth.

**1996 13" vinyl F.A.O. Schwarz "Skippy,"
$92.00.** *Courtesy Lilian Booth.*

**1996 F.A.O. Schwarz 13" vinyl "Skippy"
with Skippy pin, $69.00.**
Courtesy Lilian Booth.

Dy-Dee, the "almost human doll"

Effanbee contracted with Marie Whitman who had developed a drink/wet valve mechanism that would allow a doll to "drink" and then "wet." Effanbee used the talents of Bernard Lipfert to sculpt a doll head with molded ears that was to be made of hard rubber. They contracted the bodies out to Miller Rubber Co. of Akron, Ohio. The idea of a doll wetting its diaper was considered in poor taste and the doll was rejected by Harrods in London, until one of the royal family requested one.

The doll was referred to as the "Almost Human Doll" in promotions. The doll was introduced in April of 1934, in two sizes. It soon was available with layettes and trunks or all could be purchased separately. By 1935, Dy-Dees came in several sizes, 11" Dy-Dee-Ette, 13" Dy-Dee-Kin , 15" Dy-Dee, and 20" Dy-Dee Ann, that soon became Dy-Dee Lou. Aunt Patsy was the official spokesperson on Dy-Dee care.

In 1936, there was a new Golden Treasure Chest to hold Dy-Dee's wardrobe as well as a bathinette to bathe her and a buggy to carry her places. An instruction booklet was now included with Dy-Dee entitled, "What Every Young Doll Mother Should Know."

The book *Dy-Dee Doll's Days* was featured in Dy-Dee sets in the 1937 Ward's catalog. New accessories included a diaper bag and mother outfit which included rubber apron, white uniform cap and apron, bath accessories, hot water bottle, and diary.

In 1938, Dy-Dee could blow bubbles with her bubble-pipe and sip from her spoon. A new size was the 9" "Dy-Dee-Wee." Queen Holden drew Dy-Dee Baby paper dolls that were published by Whitman. In 1939, advertising showed pink and blue name print pajamas with the Dy-Dee sets.

In 1940, Dy-Dee was redesigned to include applied rubber ears and real nostrils with holes. Cotton swabs to clean the ears and nose came with Dy-Dee sets. Now there are three sizes of Dy-Dees, 11", 15", and 20".

In 1941 the 20" Dy-Dee Lou's name was changed to Dy-Dee Louise and Dy-Dee Jane was the 15" doll and Dy-Dee Ellen was 11" tall. New, too, were blankets with Dy-Dee name printed on them. The tousle head caracul wig was new that year. Dy-Dees with striped pajamas were seen in the ads. During the war years, Dy-Dee was featured with layettes and bathinettes and as the war progresses and rubber shortages appeared, just accessories were promoted — not the dolls.

In 1946, Effanbee was sold to Noma Electric and they began offering Dy-Dee in a travel-type case with handle and lock. Also new was bubble bath in the layette. In 1948, a crier/pacifier was included in the layette and after 1948 tear ducts were added. Dy-Dee was produced in hard plastic and vinyl in the 1950s.

What to look for:

Look for Dy-Dee dolls in good condition, without all the color scrubbed off by some loving owner who may have put her doll in a bathinette or allowed water from her drink bottle to leak onto her face. Dy-Dees had wonderful wardrobe trunks and layette sets, and some are still available as well as accessories such as bottles, bubble pipes, diaries, and bathinettes. Many have deteriorating bodies, because the rubber may have cracked or heat has caused it to go out of shape. Some can be stuffed with cotton or covered with stockings if they are flaking.

11" rubber "Dy-Dee Ellen," $175.00.
Courtesy Peggy Montei.

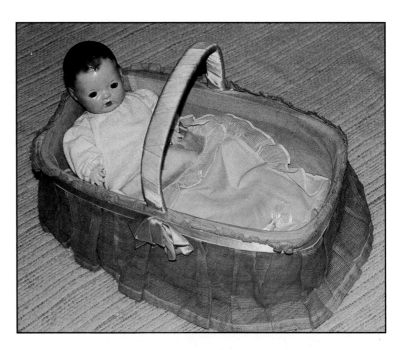

13" rubber "Dy-Dee" in basket with original mattress and coverlet, perhaps made by Effanbee, $200.00.
Courtesy Peggy Montei.

15" rubber "Dy-Dee Jane," $225.00; 20" "Dy-Dee Louise," $300.00; 11" "Dy-Dee Ellen," $175.00. *Courtesy Louise M. Lunde.*

11" "Dy-Dee" with original christening dress, slip, hat, sleepers, and bathrobe, wardrobe box, $425.00. *Courtesy Peggy Montei.*

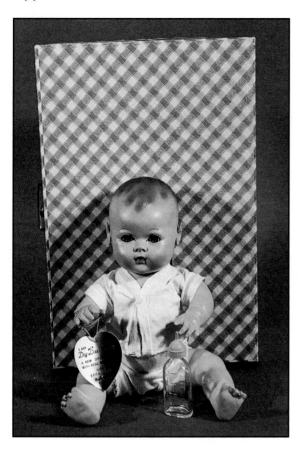

15" "Dy-Dee Jane," hard plastic head, rubber body, applied ears, suitcase has three-piece outfit, accessories, $300.00.
Courtesy Angie Gonzales.

15" rubber "Dy-Dee Baby," caracul wig, $175.00. *Courtesy Iva Mae Jones.*

20" "Dy-Dee Louise," $250.00; and 15" "Dy-Dee Jane," $175.00; with Dy-Dee Dolls Days book, $50.00 – 75.00.
Courtesy Barbara Cresenze.

11" "Dy-Dee Ellen" with accessories, $200.00.
Courtesy Pat Schuda.

20" "Dy-Dee Louise," with applied ears, $250.00. *Courtesy Barbara Cresenze.*

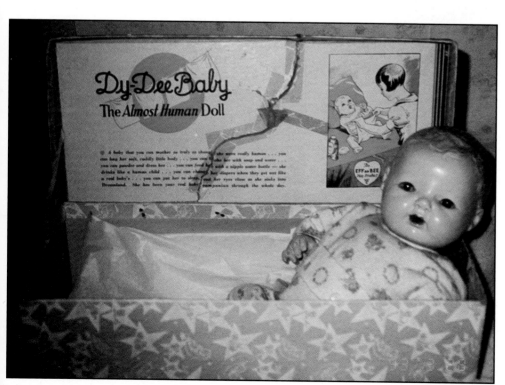

15" "Dy-Dee Baby," early model with molded on ears, in box, $250.00.
Courtesy Barbara Cresenze.

Ethnic Dolls

Ethnic dolls refer to dolls in regional costumes — a category that has been overlooked by many more sophisticated collectors who concentrate on more well-researched dolls. Dolls in national costumes were made of many mediums, including bisque, cloth, composition, hard plastic, and vinyl. During the 1930s, 1940s, 1950s, and later, many dolls dressed in regional costumes could be purchased cheaply as souvenirs in different areas. A wide variety of these dolls are unmarked or made by little known companies. This category is sometimes a catchall for dolls that have little history. Many were cheaply made and mass produced for the tourist market, but some were extremely well made and are whimsical and charming and make an interesting and eclectic collection.

What to look for:

Look for clean all original dolls with boxes, labels, and/or tagged clothing. Try for dolls with well made clothing that is clean with bright colors and no fading or soil. This category has great potential since dolls of little known or unknown manufacturers may be passed by.

Acquire dolls that are appealing to you, but always look for well made dolls with good and original costumes.

16" unmarked cloth dolls in German costume, googly eyes, $350.00+ for pair.
Courtesy Mary Evelyn Graf.

13" clay Santon wood carrier, by S. Jouglas, Provence, France, $60.00.
Courtesy Cherie Gervais.

9" clay Santon Fisherman, $55.00.
Courtesy Cherie Gervais.

**9" French Santon made by Amy,
wood gatherer, $40.00.**
Courtesy Cherie Gervais.

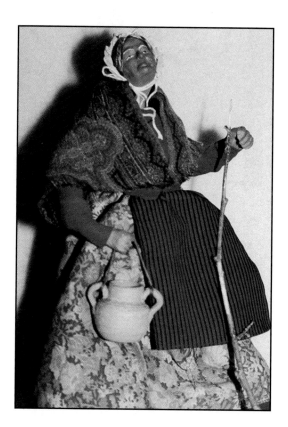

**Clay Santon water carrier,
by S. Jouglass, Provence, France, $55.00.**
Courtesy Cherie Gervais.

**10" cloth doll with pipe, original clothes,
Hungarian costume, $50.00.**
Courtesy Cherie Gervais.

8½" French cloth doll with painted features, cloth covered metal armature body, metallic floss hair, hand attached to metal dog (a heavy accessory), **$65.00.** *Courtesy Joanna Smith.*

13" Skookum's Chief and 12½" Squaw composition pair with blanket covered bodies, Squaw carries papoose, painted features, **$400.00 pair.** *Courtesy Timothy Smith.*

13" leather Native American doll with floss hair, beads for eyes and mouth, leather beaded costume, presumed cottage industry doll made for sale to tourists, **$50.00.** *Courtesy Fern Pilley.*

Hard Plastic

Plastics came into use during World War II. The war and shortages of some materials caused great upheavals in the toy industry as some plants had been converted to make items for the war effort. After the war, some companies began to use plastic for dolls. Hard plastic seems to have been a good material for doll use. Relatively unbreakable, it seems not to deteriorate with time, such as the "magic skin" and other materials that were tried and discarded. The prime years of use, roughly a ten year period (circa late 1940s – 1950s), produced a wide variety of beautiful dolls that Baby Boomers still remember fondly. With the advent of vinyl, in the late 1950s and early 1960s, less hard plastic dolls were made, although occasionally some manufacturer still presents hard plastic today.

What to look for:

Look for clean dolls with rosy cheek color, original clothing, labels, boxes, hang tags, or brochures. Dirt may have caused the plastic to change chemically with the growth of bacteria when the relative humidity is high. Another way for collectors to find inexpensive dolls is to look for those that are unmarked or by little known companies.

11" Doll's Paradise, NY, "Davy Crockett" with sleep eyes, closed mouth, all original, unmarked, wears ribbon marked Crockett, in box, $125.00.
Courtesy Julie Marthaller.

Hard Plastic

18" "Mary Lu Walker" with wrist tag (left) that reads "Mary Lu Walker//Doll Bodies//Inc.//N.Y. 12 N.Y.," $275.00.
Courtesy Ursula Mertz

14" all original doll, saran hair, hang tag reads "Your //A.B.C. Dolly//with//Saran//Hair//Combed — Curled//Waved," $275.00+. *Courtesy Ursula Mertz.*

4½" "Saturday's Baby"
of the Everyday Series by Hollywood Dolls,
$45.00. *Courtesy Imogene Hunt.*

9" English Cottage Doll, cloth body and arms, face
looks to be hard plastic, $75.00.
Courtesy Cherie Gervais.

13" Furga child, sleep eyes, orig-
inal outfit, ca. 1940s – 50s,
$125.00.
Courtesy Peggy Viskocil.

5" all original, boxed "Sweet Spirit" of the Playmate
Series, Hollywood Doll Manufacturing Co.,
$65.00.
Courtesy Faye Newberry.

8½" all original with tag,
mohair wig, painted eyes,
shoes and socks, $50.00.
Courtesy Sue Kinkade.

14" Roberta "Bride," in labeled box,
sleep eyes, eye shadow,
$395.00. *Courtesy Sally McVey.*

18" Doll Bodies Inc. "Mary Lu
Walker," blond wig, blue sleep
eyes, unmarked, hang tag, original dress, $150.00.
Courtesy Sue Robertson.

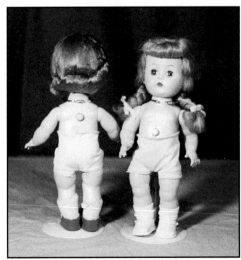

11½" "Karen, the Answer Doll" by Block,
ca. 1957 – 1958, dressed with box, also undressed, $85.00.
Courtesy Imogene Hunt and Louise Stanton

Hasbro: JEM

Jem dolls were produced by Hasbro in 1985 and 1986. They were patterned after characters in the Jem cartoon series which aired from 1985 to 1988 and was later available as reruns. The complete line of Jem dolls consists of only 21 dolls, but there are a lot of variations and rare fashions to keep the collector hunting. All dolls are 12" tall (except Starlight who is 11"), totally posable as the knees and elbows bend and the waist and head turn and the wrists swivel, and are realistically proportioned like a human figure. They are made of vinyl with rooted hair. They are marked on head "Hasbro, Inc." Some backs are marked "COPYRIGHT 1985 HASBRO, INC.//CHINA" and some are marked "COPYRIGHT 1987 HASBRO//MADE IN HONG KONG." Starlight girls are unmarked. The exciting thing about Jem dolls and the appeal to the public may have been the "truly outrageous" flashy mod fashions and startling hair colors available that made them so different from other fashion-type dolls of this era.

What to look for:

Check those outrageous fashions you find loose — they could belong to Jem. Dolls should be clean, with no fading, good color, and with boxes, cards, or brochures. A great niche collectible that appeals to those who got the dolls as gifts and those who love the fashions.

"Jem-Jerrica" (1st issue Jem) wearing **"Only The Beginning"** of the On Stage Fashions (one of the easiest outfits to still find), $20.00.
Courtesy Linda Holton.

Left: "Rock 'n Curl Jem" wearing casual side of Flip Side Fashion **"We Can Change It."** **Right: "Shana"** wearing dress-up side of Flip Side Fashion **"We Can Change It."** Fashion mint and complete, $75.00. Nude mint Rock'n Curl Jem, $7.00; nude mint 1st issue Shana, $35.00. *Courtesy Linda Holton.*

Hasbro: Jem

Left: "Pizzazz" wearing Smashin' Fashion "You Can't Catch Me." Fashion mint and complete, $25.00, mint nude 1st issue Pizzazz, $15.00. Right: "Roxy" wearing Smashin' Fashion "Let The Music Play." Fashion mint and complete, $20.00, mint nude 1st issue Roxy, $15.00.
Courtesy Linda Holton.

Left: "Shana," wearing On Stage Fashion "Music is Magic." Mint/complete fashion $20.00, mint nude 1st issue Shana $35.00. Right: "Shana" wearing On Stage Fashion "Love's Not Easy." Mint/complete fashion $50.00, mint nude 1st issue Shana, $35.00.
Courtesy Linda Holton.

"Raya," left, wearing Music Is Magic Fashion "Rhythm & Flash." Outfit mint and complete, $22.00, Raya mint nude, $35.00. 1st Issue "Kimber," right, wearing Music is Magic Fashion "Rock'n Roses." Outfit mint and complete, $26.00, mint nude 1st issue Kimber, $10.00.
Courtesy Linda Holton.

Left: "Raya" wearing Flip Side Fashion "Rock Country."
Mint and complete Rock Country, $22.00,
nude mint Raya, $35.00.
Right: 1st issue "Aja" wearing Flip Side Fashion
"Sophisticated Lady" with blouse and sunglasses shown at
feet. Complete Sophisticated Lady, $15.00;
mint nude 1st issue Aja, $15.00.
Courtesy Linda Holton.

Left: 1st issue "Rio" wearing "Rappin" issued first as a
Smashin' Fashion and then as a Rio Fashion. Mint/complete
Rappin fashion only, $15.00; mint nude 1st issue Rio, $10.00.
Right: "Glitter 'n Gold Rio" wearing Rio Fashion "Share A
Little Bit." Mint/complete Share A Little Bit fashion only,
$55.00; mint/nude Glitter 'n Gold Rio, $10.00.
Courtesy Linda Holton.

Left: "Roxy" wearing Smashin' Fashion "Just
Mishbehavin." Mint complete fashion only,
$45.00+, mint nude 1st issue Roxy, $15.00.
Right: "Roxy" wearing Smashin' Fashion
"There Ain't Nobody Better." Mint/complete
fashion $40.00; mint/nude 1st issue Roxy,
$15.00. *Courtesy Linda Holton.*

Hitty

Hitty is a character in the book, *Hitty, Her First Hundred Years* by Rachel Field, published in 1929. It is a story of a 6" doll, Hitty, and her adventures through 100 years. The story remains popular with people who read it as children and give the book to their children and grandchildren. It is charmingly illustrated with pen and ink drawings and early editions also contain some color plates. The original Hitty makes her home in the library in Sturbridge, MA, while today's artists re-create Hitty for collectors. A Hitty newsletter is published and Hitty get-togethers happen at doll conventions and conferences. See Collectors' Network for information on the Hitty newsletter to keep abreast of latest artist creations.

What to look for:

Reread the Hitty book to fix in your mind your ideal Hitty and then look for the many artists' interpretations available today. You can find them nude or dressed giving you options on price and the opportunity to make a wardrobe for your own Hitty. You may wish to try carving your own.

**The original "Hitty," subject of the 1929 book *Hitty,
Her First Hundred Years,* by Rachel Field, as shown at
the UFDC national convention in Dallas, TX, from her
permanent home at the Sturbridge, MA, library.**

7" wooden "Hitty" doll by Helen Bullard, marked "Holly, Ozone, TN," jointed arms and legs, $350.00. *Courtesy Peggy Viskocil.*

All wooden souvenir "Hitty in the Apple Orchard" 1996 Hitty Luncheon, UFDC National Convention, Dallas, TX, $125.00. *Courtesy Martha Cramer.*

6" wooden doll, hand carved by Larry Tyckson, dressed by Lois Tyckson, marked Larry Tyckson (son-in-law) of Sherman Smith, stand included, $65.00. *Courtesy Martha Cramer.*

"Hitty" by Ruth A. Brown, Grant's Pass, OR, $175.00. *Courtesy Marian W. Pettygrove.*

Horsman

Horsman was founded by Edward Imeson Horsman in New York City. It operated from 1865 to 1980+. The E.I. Horsman company distributed, assembled, and made dolls. It merged with Aetna Doll and Toy Co. In 1909 Horsman obtained his first copyright for a complete doll with Billiken. The company later made hard plastic and vinyl dolls many of which are unmarked, some have only a number, and some may be marked Horsman. Judds report painted inset pins on the walking mechanism is one means of identification of hard plastic dolls. Some of the hard plastic dolls included Cindy with either a child or fashion-type body.

What to look for:

Composition dolls should have minimal crazing, rosy cheeks, original clothing, labels, or tags when possible. Great characters like the Campbell Kids are always charming. Modern dolls should be perfect and all original. A nifty collecting niche; collectors may find bargains as later Horsman dolls have not been as popular with collectors.

12" composition "Campbell Kids,"
in blue check outfits,
$300.00 for pair.
Courtesy McMasters Doll Auctions.

18" composition "Bye-Lo-type,"
$225.00.
Courtesy Connielee Martin.

15" rigid vinyl doll with braids, original dress,
$15.00. *Courtesy Vivian Boucher.*

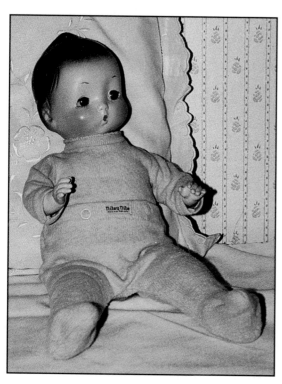

14" marked "Jeanie," ca. 1937, composition
head, arms, legs, cloth body with crier,
brown tin sleep eyes, molded painted hair,
"Nitey Nite" sleepers, restored, $250.00.
Courtesy Marian Pettygrove.

20" composition "Dimples,"
cloth torso, tin eyes, $400.00.
Courtesy Cherie Gervais.

Horsman's Peggy Ann

THE SUB-TEEN DOLL

WITH **PERMA-CURL**
MIRACLE ROOTED HAIR

- ALL VINYL
- WASHABLE • SLEEPS
- UNBREAKABLE
- JOINTED ARMS, LEGS

17" vinyl "Peggy Ann," marked "Horsman" on head and body, soft vinyl head, rigid vinyl body, rooted reddish hair, blue sleep eyes, all original with hang tag, $75.00. *Courtesy Ursula Mertz.*

HORSMAN *Peggy Ann*

- PERMA-CURL ROOTED HAIR — Not a wig. Each fibre firmly implanted in the scalp. Can be WASHED, WAVED, BRUSHED, CURLED, COMBED.
- MADE ENTIRELY of vinyl plastic. Note perfection of detail in fingers, knuckles, etc.
- WASHABLE, practically unbreakable. Won't crack, chip or peel.
- Large, sleeping eyes with long lashes.
- Fully jointed arms and legs.
- Head turns.
- Fine quality garments.

Made in Columbia, S. C., U.S.A.

by HORSMAN DOLLS, INC.

Mary Hoyer

Mary Hoyer operated a mail-order business and yarn shop and sold yarn and patterns for children's knitted and crocheted garments. She began to offer patterns for dolls and had Bernard Lipfert design a doll for her that was made first in composition and later in hard plastic. You could buy the doll undressed and make the patterned outfits for her. Hoyer also sold ready-made outfits. The dolls are marked "The Mary Hoyer Doll" or "ORIGINAL Mary Hoyer Doll." Today her granddaughter, Mary Lynne, carries on the business and produces dolls in vinyl based on an original book by Mary Hoyer, *The Doll with the Magic Wand.*

What to look for:

Mary Hoyer dolls are a great delight for knitters as they get to use all those patterns in Mary Hoyer pattern books, which have been reissued and are still on the market. Mary Hoyer dolls are a great collectible to look for in composition and hard plastic, but do not pass up the new ones. Look for rosy cheeks, little crazing if composition, clean hard plastic, original outfits.

14" vinyl "Playtime" doll, shows the attention to detail with the cute alphabet print on skirt, $79.95, retail.
Courtesy Peggy Millhouse.

Mary Hoyer

13½" vinyl dolls from *The Doll with the Magic Wand*, ca. 1990, limited edition, including the characters, "Fairy," "Paublo," "Prince Bogie," "King," "Queen," "Princess," "Tyrina," "Mandy," and book, $1,800.00 for set.
Courtesy Sue Robertson.

Mary Hoyer holding one of her dolls at a Mary Hoyer Luncheon at the Modern Doll Convention. Mary's granddaughter Mary Lynn Saunders heads the Mary Hoyer Doll Co. today. Mary Hoyer is a talented gracious lady whose patterns remain a favorite with collectors.

14" composition, red mohair wig, side-glancing painted eyes, blue knitted costume, on roller skates, $400.00.
Courtesy Stephanie Prince.

Above: 14" pair of composition dolls with pattern-made skating outfits, $350.00 – 450.00. *Courtesy Mary Evelyn Graf.*

14" composition in five-piece crocheted ice skating costume, from Mary Hoyer pattern, "Delores," auburn mohair wig, blue sleep eyes, excellent color, $525.00.
Courtesy Sue Robertson.

10" vinyl "Margie" toddler, rooted hair, blue sleep eyes, not original clothes, if mint in box, price would be $75.00.
Courtesy Sue Robertson.

14" vinyl "Becky," unmarked, came in mailing box, ca. 1967, $300.00+.
Courtesy Sue Robertson.

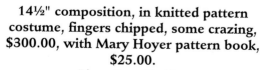

14½" composition, in knitted pattern costume, fingers chipped, some crazing, $300.00, with Mary Hoyer pattern book, $25.00.
Photo: Scott Gladden.
Courtesy Ellen Sturgess.

Mary Hoyer

14" hard plastic, original tagged dress, blonde wig, blue sleep eyes, $625.00.
Courtesy Sue Robertson.

14" hard plastic in knitted roller skating outfit with coat and hat, $395.00.
Courtesy Stephanie Prince.

14" hard plastic boy in knitted cowboy outfit from Mary Hoyer pattern, auburn mohair wig, blue sleep eyes, $600.00.
Courtesy Sue Robertson.

14" hard plastic "Cowgirl," sleep eyes, closed mouth, original wig, Hoyer pattern costume, excellent condition, pretty rosy cheeks, eye-shadow over eyes, $360.00.

Courtesy McMasters Doll Auctions.

14" hard plastic bride, all original, excellent condition, $500.00. *Courtesy Sharon Kolibaba.*

14" vinyl play doll, dressed in Mary Hoyer tagged camping outfit and tent, $150.00.
Courtesy Sue Robertson.

14" hard plastic, sleep eyes, closed mouth, wig, knit costume, trunk and five Hoyer pattern-made knitted outfits, excellent condition, $240.00. *Courtesy McMasters Doll Auctions.*

14" hard plastic "Southern Belle," sleep eyes, eye-shadow, blonde synthetic wig, original blue dotted Swiss long gown with parasol in labeled box with flyer, $650.00. *Courtesy Sally McVey.*

14" hard plastic "Ballerina" with brunette wig, one blue and one brown sleep eye, mint in box with tagged costume, $1,200.00. *Courtesy Sue Robertson.*

14" hard plastic, mint in original white box, tagged dress, brunette with blue sleep eyes, $1,200.00.
Courtesy Sue Robertson.

Ideal

Ideal Novelty and Toy Co. produced their own composition dolls in the early years (1906 – 1990+, Brooklyn, NY). Morris Michtom started the business by making teddy bears in 1906 with his wife, Rose, after the incident in which President Teddy Roosevelt would not shoot a bear cub during a hunting expedition. Michtom also began making composition "unbreakable" dolls about this time. His early comic characters were popular. Ideal also produced licensed dolls for companies to help promote their products such as Uneeda Kid that carried a small box of crackers for the Uneeda Biscuit Company. Some of their big successes were Shirley Temple in composition, Saucy Walker and Toni in hard plastic, and Miss Revlon in vinyl. They also made dolls of cloth and rubber. They used various marks including "IDEAL" (in a diamond) "US of A"; "IDEAL Novelty and Toy Co., Brooklyn, New York," and others.

What to look for:

Look for dolls with minimal crazing in composition, good color, and original clothing. Hard plastic and vinyl dolls should have very good color, and clean, bright, perhaps tagged original clothing. A wide variety of Ideal dolls are available as they were in business for so many years.

21" P-93 hard plastic "Toni," original dress, blonde synthetic wig, lovely bright rosy face color, $600.00. *Courtesy Sally McVey.*

Ideal

14" hard plastic "Toni" with original dress, box, wave set, wrist tag, red synthetic hair, sleep eyes, five-piece hard plastic body, $495.00.
Courtesy Sally McVey.

21" hard plastic "Toni," marked P-93, all original, $650.00.
Courtesy Sharon Kolibaba.

14" hard plastic "Toni," mint-in-box, rosy cheeks, $495.00. *Courtesy Stephanie Prince.*

21" hard plastic "Toni," nice color, all original, $500.00+.
Courtesy Mary Evelyn Graf.

27" hard plastic "Howdy Doody" with vinyl hands, cloth body, limbs, all original, with marked neckerchief, freckles, hinged jaw operated by string in back, $350.00. *Courtesy Ursula Mertz.*

15" hard plastic "Sparkle Plenty" comic strip character, daughter of Dick Tracy, with detached magic skin body, re-dressed, $25.00. *Private collection.*

**15" vinyl "Miss Revlon," marked
on head "Ideal Doll" and "Ideal
15 N" on body, re-dressed,
$95.00.** *Courtesy Sue Robertson.*

**17" vinyl "Miss Revlon," sleep eyes,
synthetic wig, rigid vinyl fashion-type
body, high heels, tagged dress, in box,
$300.00.** *Courtesy Sally McVey.*

**16" hard plastic "Saucy Walker,"
all original in box, with curlers
on card, $150.00.**
Courtesy Iva Mae Jones.

**16" hard plastic "Saucy Walker," crier,
pin-jointed walker, original dress,
$125.00.**
Courtesy Sue Robertson.

**15" vinyl "Harriet Hubbard Ayer,"
boxed with accessories, $450.00.**
Courtesy McMasters Doll Auctions.

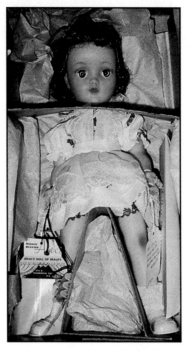

**14" vinyl "Harriet Hubbard
Ayer," in box with acces-
sories, $225.00.**
Courtesy Iva Mae Jones.

**16" black doll, "Tara,"
with growing hair, ca. 1976,
all original with box, $75.00.**
Courtesy Cathie Clark.

**Vinyl Play Pal dolls.
Left: 36" "Patti Play Pal," blonde saran wig,
closed mouth, $400.00.
Right: 38" "Peter," closed mouth, molded hair,
$850.00.** *Courtesy Virginia Lauseng.*

**15" vinyl "Velvet," all
original with box,
$65.00.**
Courtesy Cathie Clark.

Kenner

The *Star Wars* movie was made in 1977, and the sequel, *The Empire Strikes Back* in 1980. Kenner made large Star Wars figures in 1978 in Hong Kong, ranging in height from 7" to 15". They included Princess Leia Organa, Luke Sykwalker, R2-D2, Chewbaca, Darth Vader, and C-3P0. In 1979 Boba Fett, Han Solo, Stormtrooper, Ben (Obi-Wan) Kenobi, Jawa, and IG-88 were added. They also made small 3 – 4" figures starting in 1979.

What to look for:

Kenner has made a variety of modern character dolls such as Bob Scout with boy scout uniform and accessories, and sports figures and fashion-type dolls. Look for clean all original dolls with good color. Star Wars figures are more popular with toy collectors, but are always collectible, as are celebrities such as Six Million Dollar Man figures. Look for them at garage sales, flea markets, and estate sales.

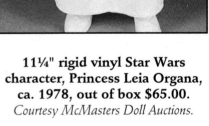

11¼" rigid vinyl Star Wars character, Princess Leia Organa, ca. 1978, out of box $65.00.
Courtesy McMasters Doll Auctions.

13½" vinyl "Cara" with rooted hair, molded purple shoes, $10.00. *Courtesy Vivian Boucher.*

11¾" rigid vinyl Star War character, "Luke Skywalker," ca. 1978, out of box $65.00.
Courtesy McMasters Doll Auctions.

Klumpe

Klumpe made caricature figures of felt over wire armature with painted mask faces in Barcelona, Spain, from 1952 to the mid 1970s. Figures represent professionals, hobbyists, Spanish dancers, historical characters, and contemporary males and females performing a wide variety of tasks. Of the 200 or more different figures, the most common are Spanish dancers, bull fighters, and doctors. Some Klumpes were imported by Effanbee in the early 1950s. Originally the figures had two sewn-on identifying cardboard tags.

What to look for:

These amusing characters may be missing their tags, but are still very collectible. Often passed over by more sophisticated collectors, they can still be found for reasonable prices. Look for those with more accessories, tags, or labels. They should be clean with bright colors. The more intricate the costume and accessories, the more desirable they are to collectors. Must be pristine with all labels to command highest prices. Keep on the lookout at estate sales, antique malls, flea markets, and doll shows for these.

11½" cloth, gold paper tag, some wear, $30.00. *Courtesy Dolores L. Jesurui.*

11" cloth "Scientist," these figures often represented different professions, $95.00. *Courtesy Gayle Elam.*

11" cloth "Fish Peddler," made in Spain for Effanbee, $95.00. *Courtesy Cherie Gervais.*

Knickerbocker

Knickerbocker Toy Co. Inc. has made a variety of celebrity dolls among others. The celebrities include two versions of Annie, from the stage play based on "Little Orphan Annie," and Daddy Warbucks, Punjab, Miss Hannigan, and Molly; Laura and Carrie from the TV version of Laura Ingalls's *Little House on the Prairie*; Mr. Spock, and Captain Kirk from the TV sci-fi series, *Star Trek,* and comedians Laurel and Hardy, W.C. Fields, and Soupy Sales. One version of Annie is based on the actress Andrea McArdle, circa 1977. It is a 15 inch all-cloth doll with jointed arms and legs, orange yarn hair, painted features, and her dog Sandy in the pocket of her red dress.

What to look for:

Disney characters such as these are highly sought after, and you just never know where they will turn up. Keep your eyes open for clean dolls, with good, bright colors. Having their hang tags and mint condition will add to the value.

10" vinyl "Pinocchio," $900.00; and 10" "Jiminy Cricket,"
$1,100.00, all original with hang tags.
Courtesy McMasters Doll Auctions.

Lawton

Wendy Lawton was born in San Francisco, and attended and graduated from California schools. There, she met and married her husband, Keith, and made her home in Turlock, California, with their two children Rebecca and Patrick. Her interests have developed around her home and her own artistic achievements. She was guided early on by doll maker Thelma Hanke who taught her all phases of doll making including making wigs, costuming, and fabrics.

Wendy is an avid reader and has been inspired by children's literature and classics to bring to life her own dolls. The family company has greatly expanded, but is still overseen by Wendy who designs, sculpts, and paints all prototypes, designs their costumes, and does some painting on the final dolls. Wendy enjoys the challenge of researching each new subject by reading and conceptualizing the character before designing the doll. Lawton's Josephine, the souvenir doll for the UFDC Region 2 North Conference in Modesto was a big hit, and quickly more than doubled the registration fee in price. The companion piece was a suitcase with extra garments, exquisitely made, as are all of the special accessories that accompany Lawton dolls.

Lawton is a 1996 DOTY Award nominee for Katherine and her Kathe Kruse Doll, Phoebe Preble and Hitty, June Amos and Mary Anne, and The Scarlet Letter. See Collectors' Network for information on the Lawton Collectors' Guild.

What to look for:

The great workmanship on Lawton dolls with wonderful wardrobe and accessories make this very modern doll a collectible that seems sure to increase in value. You may wish to add them to your collection just because you like them. These porcelain dolls sometimes turn up at doll shows still at reasonable prices. They are generally not large dolls, often under 14" tall.

Wendy Lawton's attention to detail and excellent workmanship shows in the 12" porcelain "Josephine" souvenir doll from UFDC 2 North Regional, Modesto, CA, includes suitcase and extra wardrobe, $1,250.00. *Private collection.*

Marx

Marx made tin mechanical toys, and later sets with numerous small plastic figures, and still later articulated figures of rigid vinyl, including the Johnny West action figures, circa 1965 – 1975. These were advertised in Sears catalogs. Other articulated figures made by Marx include celebrities Daniel Boone, Davy Crockett, Dwight D. Eisenhower, General Custer, Geronimo, and the Sundown Kid. Marx also made the Bold Vikings Series, including Brave Erik and Odin advertised as "movable Vikings." The articulated Vikings, complete with weapons, gear, and wearing apparel, also came boxed with horse with nodding head and rolling wheels. Erik had blond hair and green molded on clothing, while Odin had brown hair and beard and wore tan molded clothing. Marx also made the articulated Noble Knight Series with Gordon, the Gold Knight, and Sir Stuart, the Silver Knight, circa 1967. Gordon wore bronze colored clothing and had brown hair and beard, while Sir Stuart had silver molded on clothing and a black goatee, mustache, and hair. Both came with accessories.

What to look for:

Marx action figures can still be found at garage sales, estate sales, and auctions mixed in with other toys. Remember they all came with accessories and try to find the extras when you come across them.

11½" vinyl articulated action figure, "Brave Erik, the Movable Viking," circa 1967, molded blond hair, molded green clothing, missing hand, $15.00. *Courtesy Virginia Miller.*

Mattel, Inc.

Mattel was founded in 1945 in Los Angeles, CA, and has been a dominant force in the doll industry with their Barbie, Chatty Cathy, and others. The company began when Ruth and Elliott Handler and their friend Harold Matson founded the Mattel company. The name came from "Matt" for Matson and "el" for Elliot. They began by first making picture frames, evolving into toy furniture. Mattson left the company because of ill health and Ruth Handler began to handle marketing. She advertised in 1955 on a children's TV show, *The Mickey Mouse Club*. In 1959, they marketed Barbie, named after their daughter, and the company prospered. Barbie (see separate section) has become the number one collectible doll in the world. Mattel also has manufactured quite a list of celebrity dolls as well as characters from TV shows. The Handlers are no longer associated with the company.

What to look for:

These modern vinyl and hard plastic dolls are very collectible because so many kids played with them. Look for those still with boxes and accessories.

One of a kind "Snow White," designed by Lisa Temming of Mattel's Disney Collectibles, wears dress of silk, satin, and velvet, black cape lined in red silk, $5,300.00.
Courtesy Judene Hansen.

17" vinyl "Dancerella," hard plastic body, circa 1972, spins when you hold top of head, $100.00. *Courtesy Angie Gonzales.*

Mattel

11½" vinyl one-of-a-kind "Belle" from *Beauty and the Beast*, designed by Lisa Temming, 1996 Disney World Bear and Doll Convention, $5,400.00.
Courtesy Judene Hansen.

Official bedroom furniture of Mattel's "Tutti" or "Todd" dolls by Susy Goose, rigid vinyl white bed and rocker and hat rack, $795.00. *Courtesy Gayle Elam.*

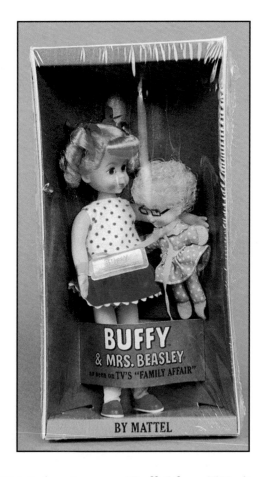

10½" vinyl Talking "Buffy" and "Mrs. Beasley" with rooted blonde hair, painted blue eyes, pull string in plastic torso, vinyl arms and legs, circa 1969, $200.00 .
Courtesy McMasters Doll Auctions.

6¼" Anissa Jones as "Buffy" from T.V. sitcom, *Family Affair*, all vinyl, one-piece body, with wire armature so body can pose, rooted blonde hair, painted blue eyes, $100.00.
Courtesy McMasters Doll Auctions.

Mego

Mego Corp. made a huge slate of action figures, comic figures, and celebrity dolls including the "Our Gang" characters; Batman, Robin, the Joker, and Batgirl; Dorothy, The Tinman, Glinda the Good Witch, The Cowardy Lion, and the Scarecrow from *The Wizard of Oz*; The Captain and Tenille; Diana Ross; Davy Crockett; Captain James Kirk, Dr. McCoy, Mr. Spock, Mr. Scott, Lt. Uhura; Farah Fawcett; Flash Gordon; Broadway Joe Namath; Buck Rogers; Johnboy and the Walton characters; *M.A.S.H.* characters; *Happy Days* characters, Ritche, Ralph, and Fonzie; Superman; Spiderman; Wild Bill Hickok; and Wonder Woman.

What to look for:

A wide variety of celebrity dolls and characters hit the hot button of those "boomers" that remember television and sports personalities like these. Look for clean all original dolls with good, bright colors. Still readily available at doll shows, flea markets, and garage sales.

Above: 12" vinyl "Growing Hair Cher," $25.00.
Courtesy Janet Santacruce.

Left photos: 13" vinyl "Cher," long black hair, eyelashes, painted eyes, jointed wrists, in red and silver beaded Bob Mackie dress, $160.00.
Private collection.

Nancy Ann Storybook

Nancy Ann Storybook Dolls was started in 1936, in San Francisco, CA, by Rowena Haskin (Nancy Ann Abbott). The dolls were painted bisque with mohair wigs and painted eyes. Their heads were molded to their torsos, and they had jointed limbs. They either had a sticker on their outfit or a hang tag. They also made a hard plastic 8" Muffie and 18" Miss Nancy Ann Style Show and an 11" Debbie and 7½" Lori Ann with vinyl heads and hard plastic bodies. In the 1950s and 1960s they made 10½" Miss Nancy Ann and Little Miss Nancy Ann, vinyl high-heeled fashion-type dolls.

What to look for:

The newer dolls need to be complete and mint. That is what collectors are looking for. In competition, the older, rare, mint, original, and beautiful doll is the one that catches the judges' eyes. That leaves a lot of played with and soiled dolls with faded clothing or missing accessories that are still collectible, and perhaps you can salvage some great dolls that others have skipped over. You can certainly find enough to collect, but always look for the one with the more intricate costume, prettier coloring, and original clothing, tags, labels, or in boxes.

5" painted bisque, molded sock "Lucy Locket" with locket (original and hard to find locket), $275.00.
Courtesy Elaine Pardee.

5" painted bisque, slim "Portuguese" with jointed legs, wrist tag, no box, $325.00.
Courtesy Elaine Pardee.

5" painted bisque "Lassie Fair, #178" with gold wrist tag, black shoes, no socks, in white box with fuchsia dots, brochure, $50.00. *Courtesy Roberta Nichols.*

8" painted bisque "Boy Blue" in blue dot box, brochure, gold foil tag, $35.00.
Courtesy Faye Newberry.

5" hard plastic #75 "Debut" with black sleep eyes, wrist tag and box, from the Commencement Series, $75.00.
Courtesy Elaine Pardee.

Nancy Ann Storybook

5" hard plastic, #305 "New Moon," painted eye, mint in box, with tag, from the Operetta Series, $125.00.
Courtesy Elaine Pardee.

Five 8" hard plastic, "Muffie" dolls, first four on left ca. 1953, straight leg, non-walker, painted lashes, $175.00 each; far right, 1954 walker, molded lash, brows, $150.00.
Courtesy Peggy Millhouse.

8" hard plastic, "Muffie," molded lash walker, all original and complete, $250.00.
Courtesy Peggy Millhouse.

8" hard plastic, strung "Muffie," left to right: blue dress variation of #508, replaced shoes; "Valentine"; and white dress, another variation of #508-1, replaced shoes, $175.00 each.
Courtesy Peggy Millhouse.

8" vinyl "Muffie" molded lash walker, ca. 1956, $175.00.
Courtesy Peggy Millhouse.

10½" vinyl "Miss Nancy Ann" in original tagged dress, high heels, marked "Nancy Ann" on head, $85.00.
Courtesy Sally McVey.

17" Nancy Ann "Style Show," hard plastic non-walker, with wrist booklet, #2403 "Sweet & Lovely," $600.00. *Courtesy Elaine Pardee.*

17" hard plastic Nancy Ann "Style Show" in original ball gown with gold hang tag, lovely coloring, $800.00.
Courtesy Barbara DeFeo.

Nodders

Nodders are two-piece dolls usually made of bisque with an unjointed body and separate head attached with elastic or weighted with wire and weights to make the head swing or nod. They are usually very small, and often based on comic strip characters. They are marked Germany, Japan, or unmarked.

What to look for:

Clean, with no paint rubs, flakes, or chips. They still can be found at flea markets, antique malls, and estate sales, and are usually more sought after by toy collectors than doll collectors. Charming when found in good condition, they make a terrific collectible, ideal for small spaces.

3¼" all bisque, left to right: girl in white coat with flower, marked "Germany," $75.00; girl in blue jumper, immobile, marked "Germany," $50.00; girl in red dress and hat, marked "Germany," $75.00; boy with black suspenders, orange cap, $85.00; and girl in red skirt, blue top, yellow hat, $65.00. *Courtesy Nancy Laurenouics.*

Left: 3¼" black boy with red suspenders, marked "Germany" on feet, $150.00; right: 2¾" Moritz-type character boy with blue shirt, $125.00.
Courtesy Nancy Laurenouics.

Left to right: all bisque, 3½" "Ambrose Potts" by Solhess © Germany, $200.00; 3½" "Old Timer" by Sidney Smith © Germany, $200.00; 3¼" "Ma Winkle" by Branner, Germany, $200.00; 3¼" "Mr. Bailey, the Boss," Germany, $225.00. *Courtesy Nancy Laurenouics.*

Nodders

Left to right: 4" "Perry Winkle," copyright Germany by M.M. Branner, $225.00; 3¾" "Pa Winkle," by Branner © Germany, $225.00; 3½" "Chow Chow," Germany, $175.00; "Delong Jones," by Solhess © Germany, $225.00; 2½" "Josie," by Carl Ed Germany, $150.00; 2¾" "Junior Hebb" by Solhess © Germany, $150.00. *Courtesy Nancy Laurenouics.*

Left to right: all bisque nodders, 3¾" "Pop Jenks," Carl Ed © Germany, $225.00; 3½" "Lillums," by Carl Ed, Germany, $200.00: 3¾" "Uncle Walt," Germany, $225.00; 3½" "Mr. Wisker," by King © Germany, $200.00; 2¾" "Skeezix," Germany, $175.00; 3¾" "Rachel," Germany, $275.00. *Courtesy Nancy Laurenouics.*

Left to right: all bisque nodders, 2½" "Mickey McGuire," copyright by Fontaine Fox Germany, $175.00; 3½" "Avery," by King © Germany, $225.00; 3½" "Min," Germany, $185.00; 3½" "Doc," by King © Germany, $200.00; 3¾" "Bill," by King ©, $225.00. *Courtesy Nancy Laurenouics.*

Left to right: all bisque, 2" unmarked, boy in red suit, $85.00; 2" unmarked immobile, $55.00; 3" clown, unmarked immobile head, jointed arms, $75.00; 2¾" clown with jointed arms, stiff neck, $65.00; 3¼" unmarked girl, $125.00. *Courtesy Nancy Laurenouics.*

Left to right: all bisque, 3½" "Cheeri-Lee," immobile, stamped "Germany" on feet, $125.00; 2¼" "Fatso," by A. Carter Germany, $175.00; 2¾" "Perry Winkle," by Branner Germany, $175.00; 2" "Corky," by King © Germany, $150.00; 2½" "Marjory," by A. Sarter, Germany, $150.00; 3½" "Smitty," Germany, $200.00. *Courtesy Nancy Laurenouics.*

Left to right: all bisque, 3½" "Emmy," Willard Germany, $185.00; 3¾" "Moon Mullins," Germany, $235.00; 3¼" "Auntie Blossom," Germany, $175.00; 3¾" "Widow," $165.00; 3¾" "Rudy Hebb," by Solhess © Germany, $225.00; 3¾" "Fanny Hebb," by Solhess © Germany, $185.00. *Courtesy Nancy Laurenouics.*

Left to right: all bisque, 2¾", stamped Germany, girl in green coat and tam, $100.00; 3" Max type boy, $175.00; 3¼" boy with side-glancing eyes, $175.00; 2¾" unmarked girl, 85.00; 3¼" girl, marked Germany, $125.00; and 2¾" unmarked boy, $85.00. *Courtesy Nancy Laurenouics.*

Ronnaug Petterssen

Ronnaug Petterssen (Norway, 1901 – 1980) was an art student in Germany in 1929. She also traveled to Spain and other countries to study folk costumes. She became a member of the Norwegian Association for Arts and Crafts and won prizes for her doll-making abilities. Petterssen created a Norwegian doll exhibit for the 1937 World Exhibition in Paris, in 1939 her dolls were shown in the New York World's Fair, and after World War II they were shown internationally. Known for her attention to detail in costuming, she managed to include essential motifs even in smaller 8" dolls. Petterssen maintained a studio in Oslo, Norway, and utilized cottage industry workers to make costumes from the patterns she designed. The heads of the larger dolls are press molded of felt, while the smaller dolls may be felt or other materials. Dolls are not marked, but all had a blue-gold round dime-sized paper tag attached with gold thread on clothing. One side reads "Ronnaug Petterssen" and the other has a drawing of a Laplander and "Made in Norway//Vare Marke." Some smaller dolls have also been found of celluloid.

What to look for:

Petterssen dolls are noted for their quality construction, excellent workmanship, and attention to detail. Dolls range in size from 8" to 18" with painted or glass eyes, and may only have gold thread left where tag was attached. Look for those that are clean with bright colors. Again, a "sleeper" in the collectible world because so little is known of them.

18" cloth boy with rare glass eyes, $1,100.00.
Courtesy Barbara DeFeo.

Ronnaug Petterssen

14½" tagged cloth girl in regional dress,
painted eyes, $700.00 includes box.
Courtesy Elaine Beling.

Ronnaug Petterssen marked box.
Courtesy Elaine Beling.

Side view shows blue tag attached to
side of costume.

Pair of cloth dolls, 18" boy with rare glass eyes,
$1,100.00. *Courtesy Barbara DeFeo.*
16" girl with painted eyes, $900.00.
Courtesy Gwen Pogue.

**Close-up of cloth girl (from page 149)
with painted brown eyes.**

**15½" cloth boy, pressed felt face, painted
eyes, in Norwegian Hardanger costume,
stitched fingers, all original, $500.00.**
Courtesy Elaine Beling.

7" dolls in regional costumes, $70.00 pair.
Courtesy Cherie Gervais.

7" all-felt "Laplanders," made in Norway, paper tag on clothes, $70.00 for pair.
Courtesy Cherie Gervais.

12" cloth Norwegian Troll doll with painted pressed mask face, $350.00.
Courtesy Barbara DeFeo.

8½" all celluloid gnome pair, after elf-like characters created by Ronnaug Pettersen, back view shows round paper labels that read "Made in Norway," $250.00 pair. *Courtesy Elaine Beling.*

Puppets and Marionettes

Webster's Dictionary defines marionette as a small-scale, usually wooden figure as of a person or animal with jointed limbs that are moved from above by manipulation of the attached strings or wires — called also puppet. Webster's also defines "puppet" as a small-scale figure with a cloth body and hollow head that fits over and is moved by the hand; a marionette; or doll. Heads can be made of a variety of materials including wood, papier mache, composition, plastic, and vinyl.

What to look for:

This category, again, is often passed over for more conventional dolls. Look for dolls with box, instructions, all original with good color, no crazing, fading, or soil.

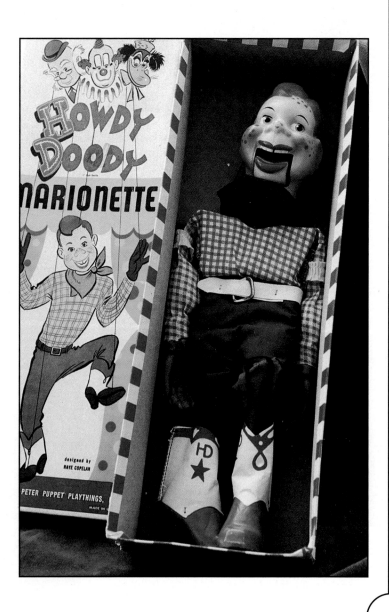

16" composition "Howdy Doody" marionette by Peter Puppet Playthings, mint-in-box, instructions on how to work puppet inside lid top, $225.00. *Courtesy Waltraud J. Hollywood.*

Quintuplets

Alexander Doll Co. won the license to produce the official Dionne quintuplets after their birth in 1934 to a Canadian farm couple. Designed by Bernard Lipfert, they were all composition with painted eyes, molded hair, and jointed baby bodies. They were also made as toddlers in different sizes. Not to be outdone, other companies came out with their own sets of five babies to try to hitch on to the selling frenzy that followed the quintuplets fame. Quint collectors have their own newsletter and collect all sorts of related memorabilia as well as the dolls. See Collectors' Network for information on the *Quint News*.

What to look for:

Dolls should be clean, bright, with good color and original clothing. Look for dolls other than Alexanders, as other companies made dolls to compete with the licensee. Other quints should not be priced as high as Alexanders.

7½" composition set of Alexander's Dionne quints in swing, tagged rompers, excellent condition, $2,300.00; 13" Alexander composition Dr. DaFoe, tagged outfit, wrist tag, excellent condition, $1,600.00.
Courtesy McMasters Doll Auctions.

Quintuplets

Five 9½" handcrafted photo-face Dionne quintuplets, $500.00.
Courtesy Connielee Martin.

5" painted bisque Armand Marseille Dream Babies, ca. 1935, in original red case with blotter, $1,000.00.
Courtesy Connielee Martin.

7½" composition Madame Alexander Dionne quints in a basket, tagged dresses, $1,600.00.
Courtesy McMasters Doll Auctions.

11" composition Madame Alexander Dionne quint toddler "Cecile" in original outfit, $375.00.
Courtesy McMasters Doll Auctions.

7½" composition Madame Alexander Dionne Quints, $1,300.00.
Courtesy Marian Pettygrove.

Raggedy Ann & Andy

Designed by Johnny Gruelle in 1915, made by various companies. Ann wears a dress with an apron, Andy a shirt and pants with matching hat.

P.J. Volland, 1920 – 34

Early dolls marked "Patented Sept. 7, 1915." All cloth, tin or wooden button eyes, painted features. Some have sewn knee or arm joints, brown or auburn sparse yarn hair, oversize hands, feet turned outward.

Mollye Goldman, 1935 – 38

Marked on chest: "Raggedy Ann and Andy Dolls Manufactured by Mollye's Doll Outfitters." Nose outlined in black, red heart on chest, reddish orange hair, multicolored legs, blue feet, some have oil cloth faces.

Georgene Novelties, 1938 – 62

Ann has orange hair and a top knot, six different mouth styles, early dolls had tin eyes, later plastic, six different noses, seams in middle of legs and arms to represent knees and elbows, feet turn forward, red and white striped legs. All have hearts that say "I love you" printed on chest. Tag sewn to left side seam, several variations, all say "Georgene Novelties, Inc."

Knickerbocker, 1962 – 82

Printed features, hair color changes from orange to red; there were five mouth and five eyelash variations, tags were located on clothing back or pant seam.

Applause Toy Company, 1981 – 83, Hasbro (Playskool) 1983+

Raggedy Ann storybooks and dolls remain a favorite with doll collectors. They too, have a newsletter *Rags* devoted to collectors, see Collectors' Network for more information.

What to look for:

Dolls that are clean, no rips or tears, original clothing, tags, or labels. Raggedy Ann was so loved that many are too worn to collect, but they are still available and eagerly sought by collectors.

31" Knickerbocker Raggedy Ann dolls, $65.00 – 75.00 each, less for one on right with incomplete costume, some fading.
Courtesy Becki Ramsey.

Richwood

Richwood Toys, Inc., was located in Annapolis, MD. Sandra Sue was produced from the late forties through the fifties. The only marks are numbers under her arm or leg. Sandra Sue was a high quality doll, similar to others produced at this time, but with more attributes than most.

Sandra Sue had sleep eyes with molded lashes, closed mouth, jointed arms and legs, made as a walker and non-walker, and had an extensive wardrobe available for her as well as a line of furniture. She had saran wigs, a suggestion of a fashion body with gently molded breasts and a slimmer waist. She was modeled with both flat and high heel feet and one tip for identification is dark orange painted eyebrows and painted lashes below eyes. The hands are formed with fingers together, separate thumbs, and the palms face in to the body.

Sandra Sue's head did not turn when she walked and her wardrobe would be the envy of many of the contemporary dolls. These included evening and bridal gowns, sports wear, such as ski apparel, skating costumes, skirts and blouses, dresses and hats, coat and dress ensembles with accessories, daytime dresses, and more.

What to look for:

Often dismissed as one of the little hard plastic dolls readily available, check your garage sales for Sandra Sue, with a collectible wardrobe made for her. Dolls should be clean, with original clothing and have good facial coloring. Her original box is easily recognizable with a silhouette in an oval and her name marked on top.

8" "Sandra Sue," hard plastic, strung, non-walker with curlers, wrist tag and brochure, $250.00.
Courtesy Peggy Millhouse.

Two 8" hard plastic "Sandra Sue" walkers seated in Pit Pat furniture, $65.00 – 200.00, depending on originality and condition. *Courtesy Peggy Millhouse.*

8" all hard plastic "Sandra Sue" in red and white striped dress, $200.00. *Courtesy Peggy Millhouse.*

Two 8" hard plastic "Sandra Sue" dolls, $225.00 each and 14" hard plastic "Cindy Lou," $200.00, all in matching original dresses. *Courtesy Peggy Millhouse.*

8" hard plastic "Sandra Sue" with flat feet in #59 blue and #41 red taffeta dresses, replaced hat, $250.00 each. *Courtesy Peggy Millhouse.*

8" hard plastic "Sandra Sue," flat foot walker, C-1 in classic felt snow suit, $185.00. *Courtesy Peggy Millhouse.*

8" hard plastic "Sandra Sue" in street dress, $175.00. *Courtesy Peggy Millhouse.*

8" hard plastic "Sandra Sue," strung, flat foot, #H-2, circa 1952, in felt spring coat and hat with wraparound dress, $250.00.
Courtesy Peggy Millhouse.

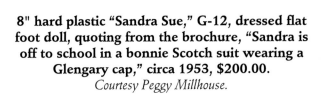

8" hard plastic "Sandra Sue," G-12, dressed flat foot doll, quoting from the brochure, "Sandra is off to school in a bonnie Scotch suit wearing a Glengary cap," circa 1953, $200.00.
Courtesy Peggy Millhouse.

8" hard plastic "Sandra Sue," #37, flat foot walker, tie shoes, circa 1954, $225.00.
Courtesy Peggy Millhouse.

8" hard plastic "Sandra Sue," in Heidi costume, mint-in-box, $350.00.
Courtesy Peggy Millhouse.

8" hard plastic "Sandra Sue" in variations of jeans outfit, if complete, $150.00 – 170.00 each. *Courtesy Peggy Millhouse.*

Richwood

14" "Cindy Lou Nurse" with box, two extra outfits, uses Mary Hoyer mold, $350.00.
Courtesy Peggy Millhouse.

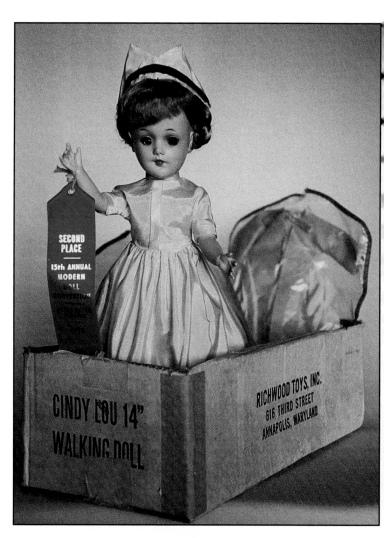

8" hard plastic "Marmee" part of Little Women group, flat foot, taffeta dress with bustle, circa 1953, $300.00.
Courtesy Peggy Millhouse.

8" hard plastic "Sandra Sue," high heel doll wearing black camisole and red skirt, $155.00.
Courtesy Peggy Millhouse.

Roldan

Roldan characters are similar to Klumpe figures in many respects. They were made in Barcelona, Spain, from the early 1960s until the mid-1970s. They are made of felt over a wire armature, with painted mask faces. Like Klumpe, Roldan figures represent professionals, hobbyists, dancers, historical characters, and contemporary males and females performing a wide variety of tasks. Some, but not all Roldans, were imported by Rosenfeld Imports and Leora Dolores of Hollywood. Figures originally came with two, sewn on, identifying cardboard tags. Roldan characters most commonly found are doctors, Spanish dancers, and bull fighters. Roldan characters tend to have somewhat smaller heads, longer necks, and more defined facial features than Klumpe.

What to look for:

Look for bright and clean doll tags; the more accessories, the more collectible these whimsical characters are.

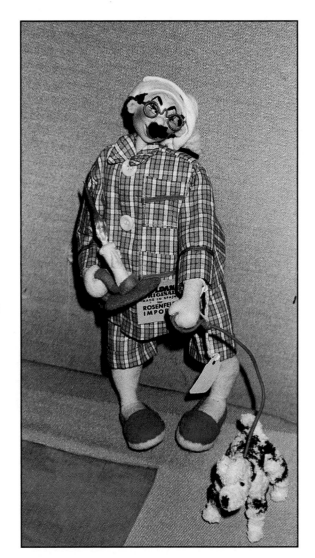

8" man in pajamas, slippers, and nightcap with candle, walking dog on leash $85.00.
Courtesy Gayle Elam.

Royal

Royal Doll Company (circa 1914+) was started by Morris Bonet. The company was bought by Rose Frankel who designed for her husband Henry Frankel. In 1964 she created Lonesome Lisa a winsome 20" vinyl doll with big painted brown eyes and rooted hair. The arms and legs had a wire armature that allowed the doll to clasp her hands, fold her arm, kneel, and make other poses. Royal dolls of this era were marked on the head "A Royal Doll" with the copyright date. In 1973, the company was bought by David and David who merged it with Jolly Toy, so you may find some marked Royal Dolls that also are marked Jolly Toy. Currently, the company is owned by "Miss Elsa," Elsa Raiji, who has designed for the company since 1951. Miss Elsa bought the company in 1977. This company makes vinyl dolls with excellent costumes — a sign of Miss Elsa's designs.

What to look for:

Check those vinyl dolls' heads for marks and copyright dates. And look for clean dolls with good color, original clothing, and tags or boxes. You may still be able to find some real bargains because dolls are often overlooked by collectors who choose more well-known products.

15" vinyl Shannon as "Dallas Cowboy Cheerleader in Formal Attire," blonde wig, sleep eyes, all original, mint-in-box, $100.00. *Courtesy Sue Robertson.*

13" vinyl "Timmy" limited edition, blond hair, blue sleep eyes, original costume, hang tag, no box, 1987, $65.00. *Courtesy Sue Robertson.*

15" vinyl "Vanessa" blonde, blue sleep eyes, "Mother's Day Series, all original, mint-in-box, $100.00.
Courtesy Sue Robertson.

15" limited edition vinyl "A Night at the Opera — Covent Garden," ca. 1989, #049, red blonde wig, blue sleep eyes, mint-in-box, $125.00.
Courtesy Sue Robertson.

15" vinyl "Crowned Princess," rooted blonde hair, blue sleep eyes, all original, mint-in-box, $125.00.
Courtesy Sue Robertson.

16" hard plastic, in original outfit and box, $200.00.
Courtesy McMasters Doll Auctions.

Sasha

Sasha dolls were created by Swiss artist, Sasha Morgenthaler, who handcrafted 20" children and 13" babies in Zurich, Switzerland, from the 1940s until her death in 1975. Her handmade studio dolls had cloth or molded bodies, five different head molds, and were hand painted by Sasha Morganthaler. To make her dolls affordable as children's playthings, she licensed Gotz Puppenfabric (1964 – 1970) in Germany and Frido Trendon Ltd. (1965 – 1986) in England to manufacture 16" Sasha dolls in series. The manufactured dolls were made of rigid vinyl with painted features. Gotz Dolls, Inc. was granted a new license in 1994 and is currently producing them in Germany. See Collectors' Network for more information on the Sasha newsletter.

What to look for:

These winsome little children are delightful to add to your collection. Sasha's dolls are found in rigid vinyl in several body shapes. The Trendon Ltd. doll has a jointed socket head, painted features, and some wear. They are unmarked except for a printed round card in a metal ring attached to doll's wrist. They have rooted nylon hair, a closed mouth, and flat feet that enable child doll to stand.

**16" rigid vinyl "Blonde Gingham"
with painted blue eyes, closed mouth,
rooted blonde hair, five-piece vinyl
body, mint; 16" rigid vinyl "Gregor" in
denims and sweater, tube wrist tags,
$225.00 each.**
Courtesy McMasters Doll Auctions.

Three body types of Sasha Morgenthaler, created in her Zurich, Switzerland, studio, include left, boy with Type A body, Type II molded head with rare molded hair; center, Type B body with Type III molded head, five-piece painted cloth body; and right, Type C farm girl with Type 1 face, ca. 1965 with molded head and five-piece molded jointed body, $6,000.00 – 8,000.00 each in excellent condition with original clothing. *Courtesy Dorisanne Osborn.*

Ca. 1965, Type C five-piece jointed molded body, excellent condition, original clothing, $8,000.00.
Courtesy Dorisanne Osborn.

16" vinyl, by Trendon. Ltd., wear colorful Sasha logo on their clothing. Gregor "School" catalog #314S and right Sasha "School" catalog #114S, typical English school uniforms, $250.00 – 300.00 each.
Courtesy Dorisanne Osborn.

16" vinyl, 1968, #4-107
"Blonde Gingham," ca. 1968 –
86, mint in tube, $500.00.
Courtesy Dorisanne Osborn.

16" #104 vinyl brunette "Red
Dress" by Trendon Ltd., ca. 1975 –
1980, silver tag, "shoebox" packaging, $275.00 – 300.00.
Courtesy Dorisanne Osborn.

16" vinyl, 1968, #5-101/4-301
"Gregor" dark "Denims" by
Frido-Trendon Ltd., gold tag,
mint-in-wide-box, $750.00.
Courtesy Dorisanne Osborn.

16" Gotz Series in ski clothing, on left
catalog #S/31/42 and right #S/11/42,
marked neck and back with Sasha logo,
ca. 1964 – 70, $1,000.00 – 2,000.00
according to condition.
Courtesy Dorisanne Osborn.

16" vinyl blonde, "Harlequin" #184A, ca. 1984, limited edition, $350.00. *Courtesy Sue Robertson.*

16" vinyl "Gregor," with red hair, corduroy outfit, ca. 1982, mint-in-box, $300.00. *Courtesy Sue Robertson.*

"Brunette Gingham," all original, $225.00. *Courtesy Margie Welker.*

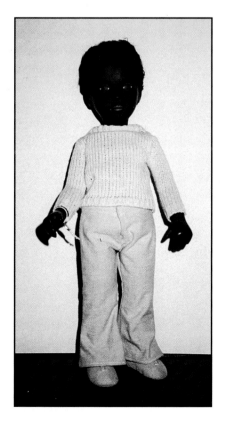

16" vinyl black "Caleb" #318, all original in white sweater and pants, mint-in-box, $300.00. *Courtesy Sue Robertson.*

16" vinyl black "Cara," #118, all orignal in floral dress, mint-in-box, $300.00. *Courtesy Sue Robertson.*

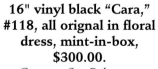

Sasha

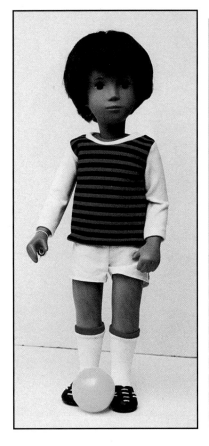

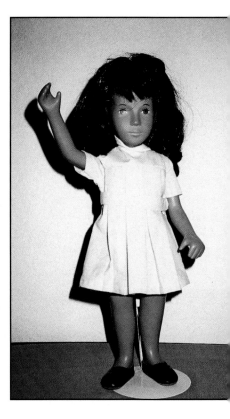

16" vinyl #303 "Gregor Dark" sport 78, by Trendon Ltd., silver tag, shoebox package, $300.00.
Courtesy Dorisanne Osborn.

16" vinyl Frido-Trendon Ltd. black dolls, left: "Cora" Cord Dress catalog #119, ca. 1985 – 86; right: "Caleb," catalog #318, ca. 1980 – 86; skin tone lightened in 1980s, $250.00 – 300.00 each.
Courtesy Dorisanne Osborn.

16" vinyl #103, brunette, pink dress, box, $300.00.
Courtesy Sue Robertson.

Vinyl "Baby Sundress" catalog #502, made 1979 – 1986 and right, Baby "Denims Playsuit" catalog #510 was made from 1980 – 1986, $150.00 – 200.00.
Courtesy Dorisanne Osborn.

12" vinyl baby in basket, #501, blonde, all original, $150.00.
Courtesy Sue Robertson.

16" vinyl blonde, #105, in blue print long dress, ca. 1975 – 80, $350.00. *Courtesy Sue Robertson.*

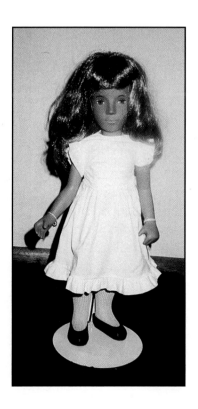

16" vinyl, #108, red hair, white dress, all orignal, $300.00.
Courtesy Sue Robertson.

16" vinyl limited edition "Velvet" (L.E. #180) by Trendon Ltd., ca. 1981, has brown wig, was the first in the series, $350.00 – 450.00.
Courtesy Dorisanne Osborn.

Shirley Temple

In 1934, after Shirley Temple stole the show with her performance in *Stand Up and Cheer* Ideal gained the license to produce Shirley Temple dolls, hired Bernard Lipfert to sculpt a prototype, cast her in composition, and soon had Shirley Temple dolls in red and white polka dotted dresses on the market. The costumes were designed by Mollye Goldman during 1934 – 1936 and show the NRA markings on their labels. The costumes were sold separately as well as with the doll. The composition dolls had sleep eyes, with some flirty eyes, open mouth with six upper teeth, multi-stroke eyebrows, a five-piece jointed body, mohair wig, and soon came in a range of sizes from 11" to 27". The first dolls were packaged with a pinback button and signed photograph. Marked on the head and/or torso, with "SHIRLEY TEMPLE//IDEAL NOV. & TOY CO." and "SHIRLEY TEMPLE" on the body. In late 1935, a Shirley Temple Baby was introduced followed by baby carriages and accessories. The Shirley Temple dolls were popular through the early 1940s, declining when Shirley reached adolescence.

In 1957, Ideal reissued a vinyl 12" Shirley to coincide with the release of her movies to television audiences and as Temple started her own television series. They have plastic script pins and paper hang tags. In the 1960s, 15", 17", and 19" vinyl dolls were issued. In 1972, Montgomery Wards, to celebrate its 100th anniversary, issued a 15" vinyl Shirley Temple. In 1982, Ideal made 8" and 12" Shirley Temple dolls costumed as Heidi, Stowaway, Stand Up and Cheer, The Little Colonel, Captain January, and The Littlest Rebel. Danbury Mint has made more recent Shirley Temple dolls, including porcelain 20" dolls costumed from movies, designed by Elke Hutchens. See Collectors' Network for information on several Shirley Temple publications and groups.

What to look for:

Composition Shirley Temples are difficult to find in excellent condition because the painted finish crazes, and so those in very good condition have risen drastically in price. Collectors may wish to search for the vinyl and newer dolls as they, too, will eventually become collectible. Check composition dolls for crazing, vinyls should have good color, and clothing should be clean and bright. Shirley collectors like all Shirley Temple related items such as marked products, paper, and advertising.

Three composition "Shirley Temple" dolls in organdy Little Colonel costumes; if all original 18" would be $1,200.00; 25" $1,600.00+. *Courtesy Glorya Woods.*

**20" composition Ideal "Shirley Temple" in cotton and organdy red dress
with cherries embroidery, reading to her bear, $1,100.00.**
Courtesy Iva Mae Jones.

18" composition Ideal "Shirley Temple"
in pink party dress from *Curly Top*
movie, shirt ties at wrists with ribbon
bows, all original with pinkback button
and box, $1,000.00+.
Courtesy Ira Mae Jones.

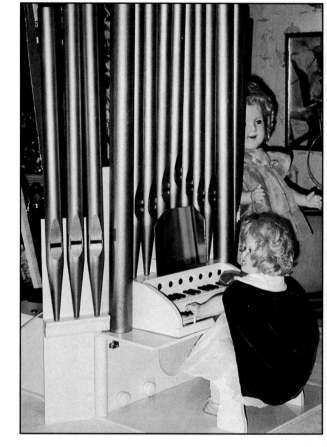

Composition store display piece,
"Shirley Temple" at the organ, $3,500.00+.
Courtesy Helen Alvis.

16" "Shirley Temple" pipe organ display,
when activated, Shirley "plays" the organ,
$3,500.00+.
Courtesy Martha Sweeney.

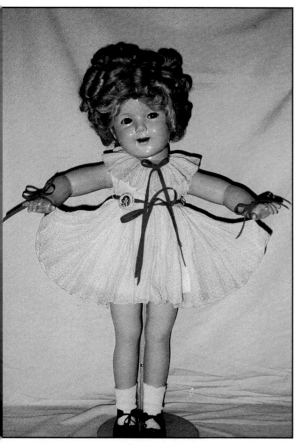

27" composition Ideal "Shirley Temple" in knife pleated party/dancing dress, ribbons tie to wrists, $1,300.00. *Courtesy Janet Mitchell.*

15" Ideal composition "Shirley Temple" in pleated party dress, all original, $750.00.
Courtesy Iva Mae Jones.

11" composition "Shirley Temple" in pleated party dress with pinback button, mint condition with rosy cheeks, clean, bright color dress has never faded or been washed, still in crisp accordion pleats, $950.00. *Courtesy Angie Gonzales.*

13" composition "Shirley Temple," original tagged party dress, $600.00; 18" composition "Shirley Temple" re-dressed in pink party dress, $650.00; and 12" vinyl Ideal "Shirley Temple" in blue party dress, $200.00. *Courtesy Diane Graves.*

Shirley Temple

13" composition Ideal "Shirley Temple" in tagged "Stand Up and Cheer" costume, trunk, hangers, extra tagged outfit, $1,800.00. *Courtesy Janet Mitchell.*

11" composition "Shirley Temple" in starburst party dress, $750.00. *Courtesy McMasters Doll Auctions.*

11" composition "Shirley Temple" in blue variation of "Stand Up and Cheer" costume, $850.00. *Courtesy Janet Mitchell.*

20" composition "Shirley Temple" in "Stand Up and Cheer" original dress, $1,000.00. *Courtesy Janet Mitchell.*

18" composition Ideal Shirley Temple, broader face, bias tape around edge of wig may indicate she is a prototype, wearing tagged coat and hat from *Poor Little Rich Girl*, $1,100.00.
Courtesy Janet Mitchell.

18" composition "Shirley Temple" in corduroy hat and coat with ermine tails costume from *Bright Eyes*, $1,000.00.
Courtesy Iva Mae Jones.

18" composition Ideal "Shirley Temple" wearing original tagged white fur coat with matching hat, $1,500.00.
Courtesy Iva Mae Jones.

177

Shirley Temple

Original advertsing shows Shirley Temple in publicity photo with doll, both wearing striped dresses from *Curly Top*. *Courtesy Janet Mitchell.*

18" composition Ideal "Shirley Temple" with broader face, bias tape around wig, may be early prototype, wearing tagged coat and hat from *Captain January*, $1,100.00. *Courtesy Janet Mitchell.*

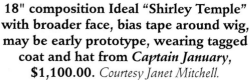

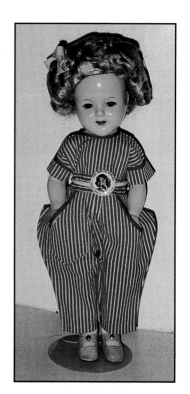

16" composition Ideal "Shirley Temple," in tagged red and white striped costume from the *Bright Eyes*, $700.00. *Courtesy Janet Mitchell.*

13" Ideal composition "Shirley Temple" in all original blue dress, tagged "A Genuine Shirley Temple Doll Dress//Reliable Toy Co. Ltd.//Made in Canada," $700.00. *Courtesy Iva Mae Jones.*

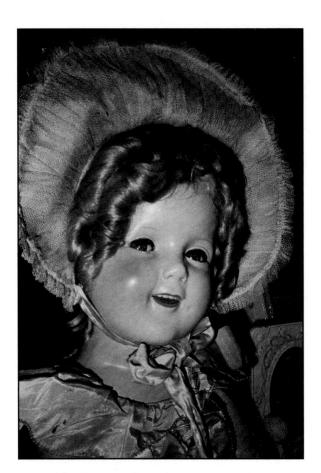

17" Ideal composition "Shirley Temple" in costume from *Little Colonel*, $1,500.00+.
Courtesy Iva Mae Jones.

18" composition Ideal "Shirley Temple" in hard-to-find complete costume from *Wee Willie Winkie*, $1,500.00.
Courtesy Helen Alvis.

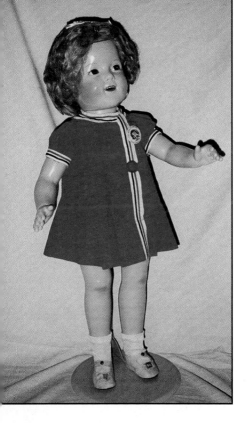

13" composition Ideal "Shirley Temple" in American Legion style coat and hat over plaid "Bright Eyes" dress from movie of same name, $650.00. *Courtesy Janet Mitchell.*

25" composition Ideal "Shirley Temple" in tagged dress from *Our Little Girl*, $1,400.00.
Courtesy Janet Mitchell.

Shirley Temple

13" composition Ideal "Marama" doll, a character from the movie *Hurricane,* using the Shirley Temple mold, even though she did not star in the movie, $590.00.
Courtesy McMasters Doll Auctions.

13" Ideal composition "Shirley Temple" in Scotty dog dress, $675.00. *Courtesy McMasters Doll Auctions.*

18" "Shirley Temple" in "Stand Up and Cheer" dress, $1,250.00 and "Snow White" in original costume, $750.00. *Photo Scott Gladden. Courtesy Ellen Sturgess.*

18" composition Ideal "Shirley Temple" with original pinback button, rare hairdo with part more to side, original dress, eyeshadow over eyes, $1,000.00+. *Courtesy Sharon Kolibaba.*

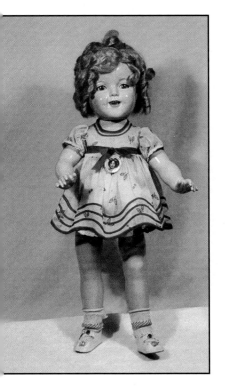

22" Ideal " Shirley Temple" in "Stand Up and Cheer" tagged dress, mint in box, $1,250.00.
Photo Scott Gladden.
Courtesy Ellen Sturgess.

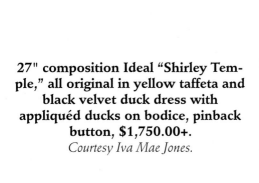

27" composition Ideal "Shirley Temple," all original in yellow taffeta and black velvet duck dress with appliquéd ducks on bodice, pinback button, $1,750.00+.
Courtesy Iva Mae Jones.

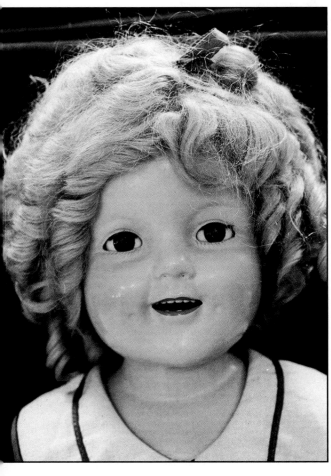

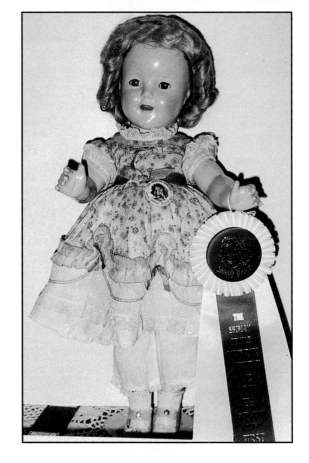

15" composition Ideal "Shirley Temple" in hard-to-find pristine costume from *Littlest Rebel*, $1,500.00. *Courtesy Janet Mitchell.*

22" Ideal composition "Shirley Temple" in "Bright Eyes" plaid dress, original pinback button, with box, $1,800.00. *Courtesy Sally McVey.*

22" Ideal composition "Baby Shirley," cloth body, re-dressed, $1,000.00, in 30" green wicker Shirley Temple buggy with her logo photo on side, $500.00+. *Courtesy Iva Mae Jones.*

18" Ideal composition "Cinderella" using Shirley Temple body, $350.00. *Courtesy Iva Mae Jones.*

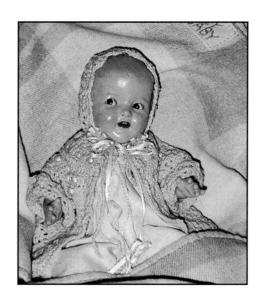

30" vinyl "Shirley Temple" baby, limited edition of 999, ca. 1985, all original by Dolls, Dreams and Love, with heart case and script pin, $350.00 – 400.00. *Courtesy Janet Mitchell.*

16" composition Ideal "Baby Shirley" marked "Shirley Temple" on head, flirty eyes, two teeth, cloth body, re-dressed, $900.00. *Courtesy Janet Mitchell.*

Shirley Temple

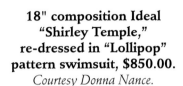

18" composition Ideal
"Shirley Temple,"
re-dressed in "Lollipop"
pattern swimsuit, $850.00.
Courtesy Donna Nance.

22" composition Ideal "Baby Shirley"
marked "Shirley Temple," open mouth,
mohair wig, original tagged dress, pinback
button, $1,500.00. *Courtesy Janet Mitchell.*

13" composition Ideal "Shirley Temple" in sailor
"Captain January" with orignal trunk and
wardrobe, $1,300.00. *Courtesy Lilian Booth.*

18" composition Ideal "Shirley Temple"
in "Poor Little Rich Girl" tagged costume,
pale color, eyes, cracked, minor crazes,
finger missing, $850.00.
Courtesy McMasters Doll Auction.

183

27" composition Ideal
"Shirley Temple" in Texas
Ranger outfit, ca. 1936,
replaced hat, $1,750.00.
Courtesy Janet Mitchell.

27" composition Ideal "Shirley Temple" Texas
Ranger with hat, holster, gun replaced,
$1,500.00. *Courtesy Iva Mae Jones.*

11" composition Ideal "Shirley Temple,"
in Texas Ranger costume made for the 1936 Texas
Centennial, mint-in-box; hat band reads "Ride 'Em
Cowboy," original pinback button, $2,000.00+.
Courtesy Iva Mae Jones.

17" Shirley Temple "Texas Ranger," boxed,
$5,000.00. *Courtesy McMasters Doll Auctions.*

11" composition Ideal "Shirley Temple" Texas Ranger outfit made for the 1936 Texas Centennial, with box, missing hat, $1,500.00. *Courtesy Janet Mitchell.*

Four 17" vinyl Ideal "Shirley Temple" dolls, left to right: in blue, re-dressed, $275.00; original yellow party dress, $435.00; original red party dress, $500.00; and original blue party dress, $435.00. *Courtesy Janet Mitchell.*

16" vinyl Ideal "Shirley Temple," ca. 1973, came in red and white *Stand Up and Cheer* dress, with extra costumes available from other movies, $165.00 each. *Courtesy Janet Mitchell.*

16" vinyl Ideal "Shirley Temple" dolls, made of very white vinyl, perhaps to give the appearance of porcelain, left to right: "Glad Rags to Riches" costume from *Baby Burlesque*; "Stand Up and Cheer" costume, and "Heidi," $150.00 each mint-in-box. *Courtesy Janet Mitchell.*

Shirley Temple

Left to right: 15" vinyl Ideal "Shirley Temple," circa 1960, in Alden's catalog, Cinderella, Bo Peep, Red Riding Hood, and Heidi, all mint, $400.00 each. *Courtesy Janet Mitchell.*

15" vinyl Ideal "Shirley Temple," ca. 1958 – 61, all original Farmerette-type costume from *Rebecca of Sunnybrook Farm*, $350.00. *Courtesy Janet Mitchell.*

18" vinyl Ideal "Shirley Temple" as Bo Peep, ca. 1960, $250.00. *Courtesy Sally McVey.*

15" vinyl Ideal "Shirley Temple" in "Alice in Wonderland" costume, blue dress with white apron, $525.00. *Courtesy Iva Mae Jones.*

15" vinyl Ideal "Shirley Temple" with
butterfly print nylon dress, sleep eyes,
rosy cheek color, $225.00.
Courtesy Sally McVey.

17" vinyl Ideal "Shirley Temple," mint-in-box,
all original, flirty eyes, pink and blue nylon
dress with orignal pin and tag, "Twinkle Eyes,"
$500.00. *Courtesy Iva Mae Jones.*

Two 36" vinyl "Shirley Temple" dolls by
Doll Dreams & Love, in bright pink costume
from *Little Colonel* and red and white dot
dress from *Stand Up and Cheer*,
$250.00 each. *Courtesy Janet Mitchell.*

Shirley Temple

35" vinyl Ideal "Shirley Temple" uses Playpal body with jointed wrists, rooted saran hair, sleep eyes, open mouth, painted teeth, all original in "Heidi" outfit with matching bonnet, $1,500.00.
Courtesy Iva Mae Jones.

36" vinyl "Shirley Temple" with jointed wrists, and box, $1,950.00.
Courtesy Angie Gonzales.

Four vinyl 12" Ideal "Shirley Temple" dolls, mint-in-box, left to right: Farmerette Rebecca, $235.00; Scotty dog jumper, $275.00; tagged print jumper, $275.00; and basic slip, $235.00.
Courtesy Janet Mitchell.

12" vinyl Ideal "Shirley Temple" with party dress and box, $250.00.
Courtesy Janet Mitchell.

12" vinyl Ideal "Shirley Temple" in cowgirl outfit, circa 1957, $200.00.
Courtesy Iva Mae Jones.

1976 Whitman "Shirley Temple" paper doll book, 1930s Cinderella frock, tagged "Shirley Temple Brand," $55.00; 8" vinyl Ideal "Wee Willie Winkie," 1982, $35.00; and 16" 1995 vinyl Danbury Mint "Dress Up Shirley Temple," retail price.
Courtesy Imogene Hunt.

8" and 12" vinyl Ideal "Shirley Temple" dolls were issued in six different costume in 1982, then later another six different costumes, $30.00 – 35.00.
Courtesy Janet Mitchell.

12" vinyl "Shirley Temple" in original dress, with tin trunk, pin, two more tagged outfits, nice color, $325.00. *Courtesy Kim Vitale.*

Shirley Temple

20" Danbury Mint porcelain with cloth body, "Shirley Temple" in red brocade "Captain January" costume, designed by Elke Hutchins, $240.00. *Courtesy Janet Mitchell.*

12" vinyl Ideal "Shirley Temple," mint-in-box, in "Wee Willie Winkie" costume, $250.00.
Courtesy Iva Mae Jones.

16" Danbury Mint porcelain "Shirley Temple" toddler with cloth body, 1996, retail price.

Courtesy Angie Gonzales.

20" porcelain Danbury Mint "Shirley Temple,"cloth body, deep yellow "Little Colonel" costume, designed by Elke Hutchins, $255.00. *Courtesy Janet Mitchell.*

20" porcelain Danbury Mint "Shirley Temple" in pink "Dimples" costume, designed by Elke Hutchins, $255.00.
Courtesy Janet Mitchell.

20" porcelain Danbury Mint "Shirley Temple" in dress up outfit from *Bright Eyes*, designed by Elke Hutchins, $255.00.
Courtesy Janet Mitchell.

16½" porcelain "Shirley Temple" Little Caroler, cloth body, green satin dress, red felt coat, $170.00.
Courtesy Janet Mitchell.

20" porcelain Danbury Mint "Shirley Temple," cloth body, lavender "Heidi" dream scene costume, designed by Elke Hutchins, $255.00.
Courtesy Janet Mitchell.

Terri Lee

Terri Lee was made from 1946 to 1962, in Lincoln, NE, and Apple Valley, CA. Dolls were first made of composition, then hard plastic and vinyl. They had closed pouty mouths, painted eyes, wigs, and jointed bodies. They were marked on torso, "TERRI LEE" and the early dolls were marked "PAT. PENDING."

Recently the molds were acquired to remake Terri Lee dolls, but the company was barred from doing so by legal action from heirs of the founder. See Collectors' Network for more information on collector groups and the bibliography for additional resource material.

What to look for:

Composition dolls are hard to find in good condition as most have crazing in moderate to severe stages. Hard plastic dolls should be clean with rosy face color and original clothing when possible. Hair can be restyled and clothes made for nude dolls. Again a stable environment and cleanliness is needed to avoid deterioration of the plastic materials.

18½" hard plastic "Connie Lynn" with painted features, long eyelashes, $350.00. *Courtesy Sally McVey.*

10½" "Tiny Terri Lee" hard plastic, painted features, long eyelashes, all original, $125.00. *Courtesy Sally McVey.*

10" hard plastic "Tiny Terri Lee" with trunk, six tagged outfits and accessories, excellent condition, $425.00. *Courtesy McMasters Doll Auctions.*

16" hard plastic "Terri Lee" original in tin, marked "Terri Lee," trunk with wardrobe, painted features, dark wig, $595.00.
Courtesy Sally McVey.

16" hard plastic "Terri Lee" with four extra pieces of wardrobe, $750.00.
Courtesy Cherie Gervais.

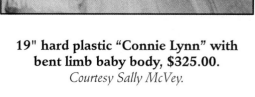

19" hard plastic "Connie Lynn" with bent limb baby body, $325.00.
Courtesy Sally McVey.

Travel Dolls

A new trend in collectibles has emerged over the past few years with the concept of the travel doll. This is a revival of an earlier concept of pocket dolls, small dolls that could be tucked into a pocket or bag and brought out when the child needed to be amused. Retired librarian, Adele Leurquin, while researching fashion articles in turn-of-the-century fashion magazines, came across an article about travel dolls. The doll was taken only on trips or excursions and put away when returning home. She brought the idea to her club and they all found small dolls and began sewing for them.

There are no hard and fast rules for the dolls, but some guidelines are mentioned. Travel dolls are usually small dolls so they can be easily carried. You may wish to choose a 4½" to 9" tall doll. Your travel doll can be of any material, old or new, bisque, hard plastic, composition, vinyl, wood, or other material. It is nice if your travel doll has jointed legs so that she can sit without a doll stand when you take her to club meetings, luncheons, conventions, or on trips. It is nice to have a container such as a trunk or suitcase to carry your travel doll, her accessories, and wardrobe. Some have been quite creative when choosing trunks; Patches, a travel bear, makes his home in his own wooden "ammo" case.

It is fun to record your travel doll's experiences in a journal so that you can keep track of what is happening to her. This concept is just for fun, a way to be creative and express your own ideas without having to conform to any rules or regulations and is particularly enjoyed by those who like to create wardrobes. Travel dolls can have a new costume for each new trip to reflect where they have traveled. Because the doll is small, it can be taken on extended trips in motor homes, trains, or automobiles. This is a concept — so you can improvise with your own personal choices and it still remains a great idea for amusing a child (or an adult) when traveling.

What to look for:

Here is where you can do your own thing. There are no hard and fast rules. You can choose any type of doll (or bear) and outfit a carrying case for her in any theme you choose.

A group of travel dolls at the 1997 UFDC annual convention were participants at a wedding of an "American Schoolboy" with bisque head, cloth limbs to a reproduction porcelain doll, with various attendants, antique to modern, including a minister bear. Prices range from $50.00 for bear to $100.00 for reproduction dolls, and antique bisque ranging from $250.00 to $600.00+.

Vinyl

By the mid-fifties, vinyl (polyvinylchloride) was being used for dolls. Material that is soft to the touch and processing that allowed hair to be rooted are positive attractions. Vinyl has become a desirable material and the market has been deluged with dolls manufactured from this product. Many dolls of this period are of little known manufacturer, unmarked, or marked only with a number. With little history behind them, these dolls need to be mint in box and totally complete to warrant top prices. An important factor to remember when purchasing vinyl dolls: all aspects of originality, labeled costume, hang tag, and box are more critical when these dolls are entered into competition.

What to look for:

Clean dolls, all original with good color, vinyl that is not sticky. There can be some real bargains in this area for the collector with a limited budget. Often overlooked character and celebrity dolls in vinyl can still be found at garage sales, flea markets, discount outlets, and antique malls.

Above: 18" unmarked fashion-type doll with good color, sleep eyes, pierced ears, high heeled feet, nicely re-dressed, $35.00.
Courtesy Eileen Honnaker.

19" Miss America by Sayco Doll Corporation, marked "14R," soft vinyl head, rooted hair, rigid vinyl body and limbs, high heeled feet, jointed waist, all original including plastic crown and box, with official entry blank for Little Miss America contest, $95.00. *Courtesy Ursula Mertz.*

Every little girl has the opportunity to become the lucky Little Miss America in this annual event.

Nothing to buy! No letters to write!

Only One Free entry blank may be entered by each girl.

Extra Special entry blanks are in every little Miss America Doll and separate outfit package. You may enter as many of these blanks as you wish.

NOTICE! Mother or guardian is responsible for correctly filling in and mailing all entry blanks.

IMPORTANT — All entries must be postmarked no later than July 27th. Any entries received after this date will be entered automatically in the next Miss America's contest.

Miss America, in person, will "pick" the lucky winners. Winners will be notified by August 15th.

Any resident of Continental United States may enter except employees of Sayco Doll Corporation, its Advertising Agency, its suppliers and their families. Prizes will be on the basis of a drawing by Miss America. Only one prize to a child. All entries become the property of Sayco Doll Corporation, New York City. This contest is subject to all local, state and federal regulations.

OFFICIAL ENTRY BLANK
Little Miss America Annual Contest
For All Girls 2 to 12

GRAND PRIZE — Free Trip to Atlantic City over Labor Day — with all expenses paid — including those of mother or chaperone.

PLUS — a beautiful costume for the winner, just like the Miss America Doll's, to wear and to own for her very own.

PLUS — the honor of meeting Miss America and participating in the Miss America festivities and pageant.

The winning Little Miss America may be a future Miss America!

50 OTHER PRIZES — for 50 other lucky girls. Each will receive an official Miss America Doll dressed in luxurious robe and gown, tiara, jewelry and holding royal sceptre.

This year's contest closes July 27th. Any entries received after this date will be entered automatically in the next Miss America's contest.

Hurry, don't delay fill in entry blank and mail today.

---- USE THIS OFFICIAL ENTRY BLANK TODAY! ----
MAIL TO: Little Miss America
Box 204
Williamsburg Station, Brooklyn 11, N. Y.

Girl's Name_____Age____
please print plainly

Parent's Name_____

Address_____

City_____

Zone_____State_____

21" Worlds of Wonder talking "Pamela" with cloth body holding cassette player, originally came with cassette and book, ca. 1986, played with condition, $50.00. *Courtesy Frances Fabian.*

23" World's of Wonder talking "Julia" played with condition, missing eyelash, $100.00.
Courtesy Frances Fabian.

10" Peggy Nesbit "Birthday Party" #3101, original dress, from My Little Girl Series, marked crossed "P & N" inside shield on body and "Made in England" and "The House of Nesbit" on hang tag, $50.00.
Courtesy Imogene Hunt.

20" "Sarah" by Maud Humphrey Bogart for Hamilton, box, button, $50.00.
Courtesy Imogene Hunt.

Vinyl

13½" baby face "So Cute Carmen" by Galoob, mint-in-box, $40.00. *Courtesy Virginia Miller.*

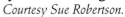

18" Shindana "Kim" with black hair, painted brown eyes, original clothes, marked on head "Shindana Toys//1978//Hong Kong," $50.00. *Courtesy Sue Robertson.*

17" strung Tomy "Kimberly" schoolgirl, ca. 1981, blonde hair, painted blue eyes, mint-in-box, $65.00. *Courtesy Sue Robertson.*

17" strung Tomy "Kimberly" black cheerleader, ca. 1983, brown painted eyes, mint-in-box, $100.00. *Courtesy Sue Robertson.*

12" "Mommy-to-be" doll by Judith Corp. IL, blonde hair, denim dress with blue and white striped inset, cap on doll's tummy lifts off to reveal removable baby inside, $50.00. *Courtesy Angie Gonzales.*

Vinyl

6½" Topper GoGo series "Brenda Brush" with flexible joints, $25.00. *Courtesy Joanna Smith.*

17" Shindana baby, open mouth nurser, orignal dress, marked on head: "C. 1978//Shindana Toys//Hong Kong," $50.00. *Courtesy Sue Robertson.*

9½" high heeled doll with original dress, rooted hair, sleep eyes, earrings, $20.00. *Private collection.*

18" Advance "Wanda Walker" with hard plastic body, blonde glued-on wig, blue sleep eyes, all original, marked "A-E" on head, rollers on feet, key wound, ca. 1950, $125.00. *Courtesy Sue Robertson.*

11½" Uneeda "Dollikin" with 14 movable joints, painted eyes, all original in box, $30.00. *Courtesy Joanna Smith.*

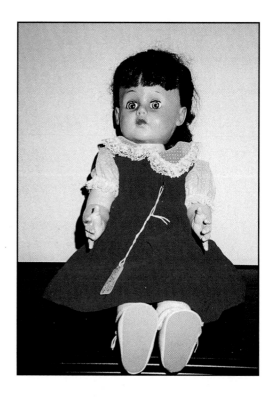

19" IMCO doll, with hard plastic pin-jointed walker body, jointed knees, blue sleep eyes, crier, dimples on hands and feet, $25.00. *Courtesy Sue Robertson.*

13½" pajama bag of bright pink and white plush, with vinyl face, $18.00. *Courtesy Eileen Honnaker.*

Vogue

Jennie Graves started the company in the 1930s, in Medford, MA, and dressed Just Me dolls in early years. She also used dolls from Arranbee and had Bernard Lipfert design Ginny. After several changes of ownership, Vogue dolls was recently purchased, in 1995, by the Wendy Lawton Company.

What to look for:

Early composition dolls should have minimal crazing and good color. Hard plastic dolls should have good color and original clothing. Hair can be restyled with patience, but clean dolls that have no mold or odor are important considerations. Vogue's Ginny dolls were a big favorite of the baby boomers during the 1950s and remain an appealing collectible.

8" hard plastic "Ginny" as Priscilla with rare red hair, silver hang tag, circa 1952, $350.00. *Courtesy Peggy Millhouse.*

8" composition "Toddles," tagged
original outfit, painted eyes,
mohair wig, bent arm, $300.00.
Courtesy Stephanie Prince.

8" composition "Toddles" brother and sister,
painted features, all original,
$350.00 each. *Courtesy Lilian Booth.*

13½" composition WAVE and WAC, circa
1940s, complete with uniform, hat, and
hard-to-find "USA" marked purse,
$500.00 each. *Courtesy Anita Maxwell.*

8" hard plastic "Ginny," Tiny Miss Series,
#42, circa 1952, wearing pink dress and
hat with replaced flowers, $250.00.
Courtesy Peggy Millhouse.

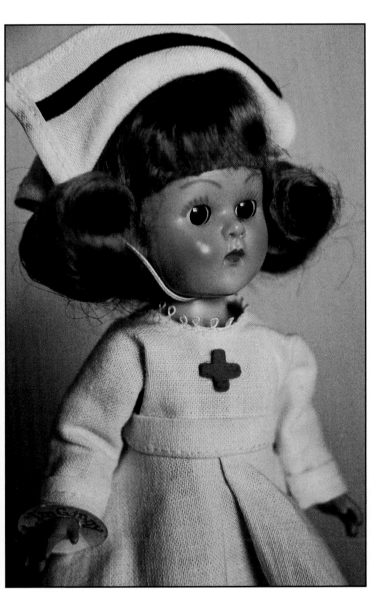

8" hard plastic "Ginny" painted lash walker, Nurse, Rain
or Shine Series, circa 1954, $300.00.
Courtesy Peggy Millhouse.

8" hard plastic "Ginny," strung, #28
Margie costume, ca. 1953, $275.00.
Courtesy Peggy Millhouse.

8" hard plastic "Ginny," circa 1952, #44 Cheryl of the Tiny Miss Series, $300.00. *Courtesy Peggy Millhouse.*

8" hard plastic "Ginny," ca. 1952, #39 Lucy of the Tiny Miss Series, $300.00. *Courtesy Peggy Millhouse.*

8" hard plastic "Ginny" in box, $225.00. *Courtesy Sally McVey.*

8" hard plastic "Ginny," painted lash walker,
Candy Dainty Series, #56, circa 1954, $325.00.
Courtesy Peggy Millhouse.

8" hard plastic "Ginny" transitional to walker,
Kay #23, replaced shoes, $275.00.
Courtesy Peggy Millhouse.

8" hard plastic "Ginny," pale
coloring, Bridal Series, $345.00.
Courtesy Stephanie Prince.

Vogue

8" hard plastic, painted eye, strung "Ginny," circa 1950, $300.00.
Courtesy Peggy Millhouse.

8" hard plastic strung "Ginny," blue and white original dress, hat, wonderful color, hang tag, $300.00.
Courtesy Sharon Kolibaba.

8" hard plastic "Ginny" with painted eyes, all original, circa 1950, #1800 series, $300.00.
Courtesy Peggy Millhouse.

8" hard plastic "Ginny," painted lash, in original outfit with tin trunk and extra wardrobe, $395.00.
Courtesy Sally McVey.

8" hard plastic "Ginny" dressed in majorette costume, tin trunk, extra wardrobe, $325.00. *Courtesy Sally McVey.*

8" hard plastic "Ginny," strung, original outfit, missing purse, #65 Angela, circa 1953, $275.00.
Courtesy Peggy Millhouse.

8" hard plastic "Ginny," strung, all original #21 Linda costume, circa 1953, $300.00. *Courtesy Peggy Millhouse.*

8" hard plastic "Ginny," strung, painted lashes, all original, with pink pique dress, silver hang tag, $400.00.
Courtesy Sharon Kolibaba.

8" hard plastic, painted eye "Ginny" brother and sister, circa 1950, $500.00 for pair.
Courtesy Connielee Martin.

8" hard plastic "Ginny," 345 Funtime,
in box, $225.00. *Courtesy Sally McVey*

10½" hard plastic, high heeled "Jill"
in incomplete outfit, circa 1957, $210.00.
Courtesy Peggy Millhouse.

8" hard plastic strung "Ginny" brother
and sister, #35 and #36,
dynel wig, painted lashes, circa 1952,
$300.00 each. *Courtesy Peggy Millhouse.*

**10" hard plastic "Jill"
with wrist tag and box, $225.00.**
Courtesy Stephanie Prince.

**10½" hard plastic, high heeled "Jill" in classic 1957
salmon stripe dress, replaced shoes, $225.00.** *Courtesy
Peggy Millhouse.*

**8" hard plastic "Muffie," mint-in-box,
$250.00.** *Courtesy Gayle Elam.*

Robin Woods

Beginning in the 1980s Robin Woods was the creative designer for various companies, including Le Petit Ami, Robin Woods Company, Madame Alexander (Alice Darling), Horsman, and Playtime Productions. Robin Woods dolls cover a wide range of mediums, though most of her early dolls are cloth. Great costuming is one factor that endears Robin Woods dolls to collectors.

What to look for:

Robin Woods is well known for her elaborate costumes and less well known for her clowns and cloth dolls. Learning to identify these early dolls enables the collector to search for some of her earlier work. Look for clean well-made cloth and clean vinyls with bright costumes.

14" vinyl "Lady Lynette," $125.00.
Courtesy Dolores L. Jesurui.

Robin Woods

18" cloth "Happy Birthday," circa 1986, $200.00.
Courtesy Toni Winder.

18" vinyl with cloth body "Kyleigh," circa 1990, $160.00.
Courtesy Toni Winder

14" vinyl "Scarlett Christmas," 1989, $265.00. *Courtesy Toni Winder.*

Reference

No one person can know it all. With the passing of time, as more and more dolls come onto the market, more and more collectors are grouping together to share their interests and are specializing in one or more categories. These are clubs or collectors who specialize in one category or type of doll who are willing to network with others. If you specialize in one of the categories listed in the price guide and want to share your knowledge with other collectors, please send us your specialty and references.

Collectors' Network

It is recommended when contacting references below and requesting information that you enclose a SASE (self-addressed stamped envelope) if you wish to receive a reply.

ALEXANDER, MADAME
The Review
Official publication of the Madame Alexander Doll Club, quarterly, plus two "Shoppers," $20.00 per year.
PO Box 330
Mundelein, IL 60060-0330
847-949-9200
fax: 847 949-9201
e-mail: http://www.madc.org

ANTIQUE DOLLS
Can research your wants
Matrix
PO Box 1410
New York, NY 10023

ANTIQUE AND MODERN DOLLS
Rosalie Whyel Museum of Doll Art
1116 108th Avenue N.E.
Bellevue, WA 98004
Phone: 206 455-1116
FAX 206 455-4793

AUCTION HOUSES
Offer absentee bidding for those who cannot attend. Call or write for a list of upcoming auctions, or if you need information about selling a collection.

McMasters Doll Auctions
James and Shari McMasters
PO Box 1755
Cambridge, OH 43725
800 842-3526 or
614 432-4419
FAX: 614 432-3191

BARBIES, MATTEL
Dream Dolls Galleries & More
Collector/Dealer
5700 Okeechobee Blvd. #20
West Palm Beach, FL 33417
888 839-3655
e-mail: dollnmore@aol.com
Jaci Jueden, Collector/Dealer
3096 Williams Hwy

Grants Pass OR 97527
Steven Pim, Collector/Dealer
3535 17th St.
San Francisco, CA 94110

CARNIVAL CHALKWARE
Thomas G. Morris
PO Box 8307
Medford OR 97504

CELEBRITY DOLLS
Celebrity Doll Journal
Loraine Burdick, Editor
413 10th Ave. Ct. NE
Puyallup, WA 98372
Quarterly, $10.00 per year

CHAT ROOMS
Doll Chat
Doll collectors' chat room that shares information, news, tips, and problems on the Internet. E-mail is forwarded to your e-mail address from networking group.
e-mail: dollchat-request@nbi.com; say "subscribe" in body of letter

AG Collector
For American Girl, Heidi Ott, and other 18" play dolls, no selling, just talk.
e-mail: ag_collector-request@lists.best.com

CHATTY CATHY, MATTEL
Chatty Cathy Collector's Club
Lisa Eisenstein, Editor
PO Box 140
Readington, NJ 08870-0140
Quarterly newsletter, dues $28.00
e-mail: chatty@eclipse.net

COMPOSITION AND TRAVEL DOLLS
Effanbee's Patsy Family
Patsy & Friends Newsletter
PO Box 311
Deming, NM 88031
Bi-monthly, $20.00 per year
e-mail: sctrading@zianet.com

Collectors' Network

COSTUMING
Doll Costumer's Guild
Helen Boothe, Editor
7112 W. Grovers Ave
Glendale, AZ 85308
$16.00 per year, bimonthly

French Fashion Gazette
Adele Leurquin, Editor
1862 Sequoia SE
Port Orchard, WA 98366

DIONNE QUINTUPLETS
Publications, Quint News
Jimmy and Fay Rodolfos, Editors
PO Box 2527
Woburn, MA 01888

Connielee Martin, Collector/Dealer
4018 East 17th St.
Tucson, AZ, 85711

DOLL REPAIRS
Zadie Carter
4331 Given
Memphis, TN 38122

Fresno Doll Hospital
1512 N. College
Fresno, CA 93728
209 266-1108

Kandyland Dolls
Rita Mauze
PO Box 146
Grande Ronde, OR 97347
503 879-5153

Life's Little Treasures
Rita Mauze
PO Box 585
Winston OR, 97496
541 679-3472

Oleta's Doll Hospital
Oleta Woodside
1413 Seville Way
Modesto, CA 95355
(209) 523-6669

GINNY DOLL CLUB
1 Corporate Drive
Grantsville, MD 91526
Quarterly, *The Ginny Journal*, club pin, membership card
800 554-1447

GIRL SCOUTS
Girl Scout Doll Collectors Patch
Pidd Miller, Collector
PO Box 631092
Houston, TX, 77263

Diane Miller, Collector
13151 Roberta Place
Garden Grove, CA 92643

HITTY
Friends of Hitty Newsletter
Virginia Ann Heyerdahl, Editor
2704 Belleview Ave
Cheverly, MD 20785
Quarterly, $12.00 per year

INTERNET
Auction sites
ebay web site:
http://cayman.ebay2.com/aw/

JEM DOLLS, HASBRO
Linda E. Holton, Collector/Dealer
P.O. Box 6753
San Rafael, CA 94903

KLUMPE DOLLS
Sondra Gast, Collector/Dealer
PO Box 252
Spring Valley, CA 91976
FAX: 619 444-4215

LAWTON, WENDY
Lawton Collectors Guild
PO Box 969
Turlock, CA 95381

Toni Winder, Collector/Dealer
1484 N. Vagedes
Fresno CA 93728

LIDDLE KIDDLES
For a signed copy of her book,
Liddle Kiddles, $22.95 post pd. Write:
Paris Langford
415 Dodge Ave
Jefferson, LA 70127
504 733-0676

MODERN DOLL CONVENTION
Cathie Clark, Chairman
2018 Kenton St
Springfield, OH 45505
513 322-3780

MUSEUMS
Enchanted World Doll Museum
"The castle across from the Corn Palace"
615 North Main
Mitchell, SD 57301
606 996-9896
FAX: 606 996-0210
Land of Enchantment Doll Museum
5201 Constitution Ave.
Albuquerque, NM 87110-5813
505 821-8558

Margaret Woodbury Strong Museum
1 Manhattan Square
Rochester, NY 14607
716 263-2700

Rosalie Whyel Museum of Doll Art
1116 108th Avenue N.E.
Bellevue, WA 98004
425 455-1116
FAX: 425 455-4793

NANCY ANN STORYBOOK
Elaine Pardee, Collector/Dealer
7909 Walerga Rd., Suite 112-213
Antelope, CA 95843
916 725-7227
FAX: 916 725-7447

ORIENTAL DOLLS
Ningyo Journal
Japanese American Dolls Enthusiasts
Shirley Funk, Editor
JADE
406 Koser Ave
Iowa City, Iowa 52246

ROBERT TONNER DOLL CLUB
Robert Tonner Doll Company
PO Box 1187
Kingston, NY 12402
Dues: $19.95
Credit card: 914 339-9537
FAX: 914 339-1259

ROLDAN DOLLS
Sondra Gast, Collector/Dealer
PO Box 252
Spring Valley, CA 91976
FAX: 619 444-4215

SANDRA SUE DOLLS, RICHWOOD TOYS INC.
Peggy Millhouse, Collector/Dealer
510 Green Hill Road
Conestoga, PA 17516

SASHA DOLLS
Friends of Sasha
$15.00 quarterly newsletter
Dorisanne Osborn, Editor
Box 187
Keuka Park, NY 14478

SHIRLEY TEMPLE
Shirley Temple Collectors News
Rita Dubas, Editor
881 Colonial Rd
Brooklyn NY 11209
Quarterly, $20 year

Lollipop News
Shirley Temple Collectors by the Sea
PO Box 6203
Oxnard, CA 93031
Membership dues: $14.00 year

TERRI LEE
Daisy Chain Newsletter
Terry Bukowski, Editor
3010 Sunland Dr.
Alamogordo, NM 88310
$20.00 per year, quarterly

UFDC
United Federation of Doll Clubs
10920 N. Ambassador Dr. Ste. 130
Kansas City, MO 64153
816 891-7040
Web Site: http://www.ufdc.org

WOODS, ROBIN
Toni Winder, Collector/Dealer
1484 N. Vagedes
Fresno, CA 93728

Bibliography

Anderton, Johana
    Twentieth Century Dolls, Trojan Press, 1971
    More Twentieth Century Dolls, Athena Publishing Co., 1974
Axe, John
    Effanbee, A Collector's Encyclopedia 1949 thru 1983, Hobby House Press, 1983
    The Encyclopedia of Celebrity Dolls, Hobby House Press, 1983
    Tammy and Her Family of Dolls, Hobby House Press, 1995
Blitman, Joe
    Francie & her Mod, Mod, Mod, Mod World of Fashion, Hobby House Press, 1996
Casper, Peggy Wiedman
    Fashionable Terri Lee Dolls, Hobby House Press, 1988
Clark, Debra
    Troll Identification & Price Guide, Collector Books, 1993
Coleman, Dorthy S., Elizabeth Ann and Evelyn Jane
    The Collector's Book of Dolls Clothes, Crown Publishers, 1975
    The Collector's Encyclopedia of Dolls, Vol. I & II, Crown Publishers, 1968, 1986
DeWein, Sibyl and Ashabraner, Joan
    The Collector's Encyclopedia of Barbie Dolls and Collectibles, Collector Books, 1977
Garrison, Susan Ann
    The Raggedy Ann & Andy Family Album, Schiffer Publishing, 1989
Izen, Judith
    A Collector's Guide to Ideal Dolls, Collector Books, 1994
Judd, Polly and Pam
    African and Asian Costumed Dolls, Hobby House Press, 1995
    Cloth Dolls, Hobby House Press, 1990
    Compo Dolls, Vol I & II, Hobby House Press, 1991, 1994
    European Costumed Dolls, Hobby House Press, 1994
    Hard Plastic Dolls, I & II, Hobby House Press, 1987, 1989
    Glamour Dolls of the 1950s & 1960s, Hobby House Press, 1988
    Santa Dolls & Figurines, Hobby House Press, 1992
Langford, Paris
    Liddle Kiddles, Collector Books, 1996
Lewis, Kathy and Don
    Chatty Cathy Dolls, Collector Books, 1994
Mandeville, A. Glen
    Ginny, An American Toddler Doll, Hobby House Press, 1994
Morris, Thomas G.
    The Carnival Chalk Prize, I & II, Prize Publishers, 1985, 1994
Moyer, Patsy
    Doll Values, Collector Books, 1997
    Modern Collectible Dolls, Collector Books, 1997
Niswonger, Jeanne D.
    That Doll Ginny, Cody Publishing, 1978
    The Ginny Doll Family, 1996
Olds, Patrick C.
    The Barbie Years, Collector Books, 1996
Pardella, Edward R.
    Shirley Temple Dolls and Fashions, Schiffler Publishing, 1992
Robison, Joleen Ashman and Sellers, Kay
    Advertising Dolls, Collector Books, 1992
Schoonmaker, Patricia N.
    Effanbee Dolls: The Formative Years, 1910 – 1929, Hobby House Press, 1984
    Patsy Doll Family Encyclopedia, Hobby House Press, 1992
Smith, Patricia R.
    Madame Alexander Collector Dolls, Collector Books, 1978
    Doll Values, Antique to Modern, Editions 1 – 12, Collector Books
    Modern Collector's Dolls, Series 1 – 8, Collector Books

Index

Index

Index

COLLECTOR BOOKS

Informing Today's Collector

For over two decades we have been keeping collectors informed on trends and values in all fields of antiques and collectibles.

DOLLS, FIGURES & TEDDY BEARS

4707	A Decade of **Barbie** Dolls & Collectibles, 1981–1991, Summers	$19.95
4631	**Barbie** Doll Boom, 1986–1995, Augustyniak	$18.95
2079	**Barbie** Doll Fashion, Volume I, Eames	$24.95
4846	**Barbie** Doll Fashion, Volume II, Eames	$24.95
3957	**Barbie** Exclusives, Rana	$18.95
4632	**Barbie** Exclusives, Book II, Rana	$18.95
4557	**Barbie**, The First 30 Years, Deutsch	$24.95
4847	**Barbie** Years, 1959–1995, 2nd Ed., Olds	$17.95
3310	**Black Dolls**, 1820–1991, Perkins	$17.95
3873	**Black Dolls**, Book II, Perkins	$17.95
3810	**Chatty Cathy Dolls**, Lewis	$15.95
1529	Collector's Encyclopedia of **Barbie** Dolls, DeWein	$19.95
4882	Collector's Encyclopedia of **Barbie** Doll Exclusives and More, Augustyniak	$19.95
2211	Collector's Encyclopedia of **Madame Alexander Dolls**, Smith	$24.95
4863	Collector's Encyclopedia of **Vogue Dolls**, Izen/Stover	$29.95
3967	Collector's Guide to **Trolls**, Peterson	$19.95
4571	**Liddle Kiddles**, Identification & Value Guide, Langford	$18.95
3826	Story of **Barbie**, Westenhouser	$19.95
1513	**Teddy Bears & Steiff** Animals, Mandel	$9.95
1817	**Teddy Bears & Steiff** Animals, 2nd Series, Mandel	$19.95
2084	**Teddy Bears, Annalee's & Steiff** Animals, 3rd Series, Mandel	$19.95
1808	Wonder of **Barbie**, Manos	$9.95
1430	World of **Barbie** Dolls, Manos	$9.95
4880	World of **Raggedy Ann** Collectibles, Avery	$24.95

TOYS, MARBLES & CHRISTMAS COLLECTIBLES

3427	**Advertising Character** Collectibles, Dotz	$17.95
2333	Antique & Collector's **Marbles**, 3rd Ed., Grist	$9.95
3827	Antique & Collector's **Toys**, 1870–1950, Longest	$24.95
3956	Baby Boomer **Games**, Identification & Value Guide, Polizzi	$24.95
4934	**Breyer Animal** Collector's Guide, Identification and Values, Browell	$19.95
3717	**Christmas** Collectibles, 2nd Edition, Whitmyer	$24.95
4976	**Christmas** Ornaments, Lights & Decorations, Johnson	$24.95
4737	**Christmas** Ornaments, Lights & Decorations, Vol. II, Johnson	$24.95
4739	**Christmas** Ornaments, Lights & Decorations, Vol. III, Johnson	$24.95
4649	Classic Plastic **Model Kits**, Polizzi	$24.95
4559	Collectible **Action Figures**, 2nd Ed., Manos	$17.95
3874	Collectible Coca-Cola Toy **Trucks**, deCourtivron	$24.95
2338	Collector's Encyclopedia of **Disneyana**, Longest, Stern	$24.95
4958	Collector's Guide to **Battery Toys**, Hultzman	$19.95
4639	Collector's Guide to **Diecast Toys & Scale Models**, Johnson	$19.95
4651	Collector's Guide to **Tinker Toys**, Strange	$18.95
4566	Collector's Guide to **Tootsietoys**, 2nd Ed., Richter	$19.95
4720	The Golden Age of **Automotive Toys**, 1925–1941, Hutchison/Johnson	$24.95
3436	Grist's Big Book of **Marbles**	$19.95
3970	Grist's Machine-Made & Contemporary **Marbles**, 2nd Ed.	$9.95
4723	**Matchbox** Toys, 1947 to 1996, 2nd Ed., Johnson	$18.95
4871	**McDonald's** Collectibles, Henriques/DuVall	$19.95
1540	**Modern Toys** 1930–1980, Baker	$19.95
3888	**Motorcycle** Toys, Antique & Contemporary, Gentry/Downs	$18.95
4953	Schroeder's Collectible **Toys**, Antique to Modern Price Guide, 4th Ed.	$17.95
1886	Stern's Guide to **Disney** Collectibles	$14.95
2139	Stern's Guide to **Disney** Collectibles, 2nd Series	$14.95
3975	Stern's Guide to **Disney** Collectibles, 3rd Series	$18.95
2028	**Toys**, Antique & Collectible, Longest	$14.95
3979	**Zany Characters** of the Ad World, Lamphier	$16.95

FURNITURE

1457	American **Oak** Furniture, McNerney	$9.95
3716	American **Oak** Furniture, Book II, McNerney	$12.95
1118	Antique **Oak** Furniture, Hill	$7.95
2271	Collector's Encyclopedia of **American** Furniture, Vol. II, Swedberg	$24.95
3720	Collector's Encyclopedia of **American** Furniture, Vol. III, Swedberg	$24.95
3878	Collector's Guide to **Oak** Furniture, George	$12.95
1755	Furniture of the **Depression Era**, Swedberg	$19.95
3906	**Heywood-Wakefield** Modern Furniture, Rouland	$18.95

1885	**Victorian** Furniture, Our American Heritage, McNerney	$9.95
3829	**Victorian** Furniture, Our American Heritage, Book II, McNerney	$9.95

JEWELRY, HATPINS, WATCHES & PURSES

1712	Antique & Collector's **Thimbles** & Accessories, Mathis	$19.95
1748	Antique **Purses**, Revised Second Ed., Holiner	$19.95
1278	Art Nouveau & Art Deco **Jewelry**, Baker	$9.95
4850	Collectible **Costume Jewelry**, Simonds	$24.95
3875	Collecting Antique **Stickpins**, Kerins	$16.95
3722	Collector's Ency. of **Compacts, Carryalls & Face Powder Boxes**, Mueller	$24.95
4854	Collector's Ency. of **Compacts, Carryalls & Face Powder Boxes**, Vol. II	$24.95
4940	**Costume Jewelry**, A Practical Handbook & Value Guide, Rezazadeh	$24.95
1716	Fifty Years of Collectible **Fashion Jewelry**, 1925–1975, Baker	$19.95
1424	**Hatpins** & Hatpin Holders, Baker	$9.95
4570	Ladies' **Compacts**, Gerson	$24.95
1181	100 Years of Collectible **Jewelry**, 1850–1950, Baker	$9.95
4729	**Sewing Tools** & Trinkets, Thompson	$24.95
2348	20th Century Fashionable Plastic **Jewelry**, Baker	$19.95
4878	Vintage & Contemporary **Purse Accessories**, Gerson	$24.95
3830	Vintage **Vanity Bags & Purses**, Gerson	$24.95

INDIANS, GUNS, KNIVES, TOOLS, PRIMITIVES

1868	Antique **Tools**, Our American Heritage, McNerney	$9.95
1426	**Arrowheads** & Projectile Points, Hothem	$7.95
4943	Field Guide to **Flint Arrowheads & Knives** of the North American Indian	$9.95
2279	**Indian Artifacts** of the Midwest, Hothem	$14.95
3885	**Indian Artifacts** of the Midwest, Book II, Hothem	$16.95
4870	**Indian Artifacts** of the Midwest, Book III, Hothem	$18.95
1964	**Indian Axes** & Related Stone Artifacts, Hothem	$14.95
2023	**Keen Kutter** Collectibles, Heuring	$14.95
4724	Modern **Guns**, Identification & Values, 11th Ed., Quertermous	$12.95
2164	**Primitives**, Our American Heritage, McNerney	$9.95
1759	**Primitives**, Our American Heritage, 2nd Series, McNerney	$14.95
4730	Standard **Knife** Collector's Guide, 3rd Ed., Ritchie & Stewart	$12.95

PAPER COLLECTIBLES & BOOKS

4633	**Big Little Books**, Jacobs	$18.95
4710	Collector's Guide to **Children's Books**, Jones	$18.95
1441	Collector's Guide to **Post Cards**, Wood	$9.95
2081	Guide to Collecting **Cookbooks**, Allen	$14.95
2080	Price Guide to **Cookbooks & Recipe Leaflets**, Dickinson	$9.95
3973	**Sheet Music** Reference & Price Guide, 2nd Ed., Pafik & Guiheen	$19.95
4654	**Victorian Trade Cards**, Historical Reference & Value Guide, Cheadle	$19.95
4733	**Whitman Juvenile Books**, Brown	$17.95

GLASSWARE

4561	Collectible **Drinking Glasses**, Chase & Kelly	$17.95
4642	Collectible **Glass Shoes**, Wheatley	$19.95
4937	Coll. **Glassware** from the 40s, 50s & 60s, 4th Ed., Florence	$19.95
1810	Collector's Encyclopedia of **American Art Glass**, Shuman	$29.95
4938	Collector's Encyclopedia of **Depression Glass**, 13th Ed., Florence	$19.95
1961	Collector's Encyclopedia of **Fry Glassware**, Fry Glass Society	$24.95
1664	Collector's Encyclopedia of **Heisey Glass**, 1925–1938, Bredehoft	$24.95
3905	Collector's Encyclopedia of **Milk Glass**, Newbound	$24.95
4936	Collector's Guide to **Candy Containers**, Dezso/Poirier	$19.95
4564	**Crackle Glass**, Weitman	$19.95
4941	**Crackle Glass**, Book II, Weitman	$19.95
2275	**Czechoslovakian Glass** and Collectibles, Barta/Rose	$16.95
4714	**Czechoslovakian Glass** and Collectibles, Book II, Barta/Rose	$16.95
4716	**Elegant Glassware** of the Depression Era, 7th Ed., Florence	$19.95
1380	Encylopedia of **Pattern Glass**, McClain	$12.95
3981	Ever's Standard **Cut Glass** Value Guide	$12.95
4659	**Fenton** Art Glass, 1907–1939, Whitmyer	$24.95
3725	**Fostoria**, Pressed, Blown & Hand Molded Shapes, Kerr	$24.95
4719	**Fostoria**, Etched, Carved & Cut Designs, Vol. II, Kerr	$24.95
3883	**Fostoria Stemware**, The Crystal for America, Long & Seate	$24.95
4644	**Imperial Carnival Glass**, Burns	$18.95
3886	**Kitchen Glassware** of the Depression Years, 5th Ed., Florence	$19.95

COLLECTOR BOOKS
Informing Today's Collector

1725	Pocket Guide to **Depression Glass**, 10th Ed., Florence	$9.95
4035	Standard Encyclopedia of **Carnival Glass**, 6th Ed., Edwards/Carwile	$24.95
4036	Standard **Carnival Glass** Price Guide, 11th Ed., Edwards/Carwile	$9.95
4875	Standard Encyclopedia of **Opalescent Glass**, 2nd ed., Edwards	$19.95
1731	**Stemware Identification**, Featuring Cordials with Values, Florence	$24.95
4326	**Very Rare Glassware** of the Depression Years, 3rd Series, Florence	$24.95
4732	**Very Rare Glassware** of the Depression Years, 5th Series, Florence	$24.95
1656	**Westmoreland Glass**, Wilson	$24.95

POTTERY

4927	**ABC Plates & Mugs**, Lindsay	$24.95
4929	**American Art Pottery**, Sigafoose	$24.95
1630	**American Limoges**, Limoges	$24.95
312	**Blue & White Stoneware**, McNerney	$9.95
1958	So. Potteries **Blue Ridge Dinnerware**, 3rd Ed., Newbound	$14.95
1959	**Blue Willow**, 2nd Ed., Gaston	$14.95
1848	Ceramic **Coin Banks**, Stoddard	$19.95
1851	Collectible **Cups & Saucers**, Harran	$18.95
3709	Collectible **Kay Finch**, Biography, Identification & Values, Martinez/Frick	$18.95
1373	Collector's Encyclopedia of **American Dinnerware**, Cunningham	$24.95
3931	Collector's Encyclopedia of **Bauer Pottery**, Chipman	$24.95
4815	Collector's Encyclopedia of **Blue Ridge Dinnerware**, Newbound	$19.95
4932	Collector's Encyclopedia of **Blue Ridge Dinnerware**, Vol. II, Newbound	$24.95
1658	Collector's Encyclopedia of **Brush-McCoy Pottery**, Huxford	$24.95
3272	Collector's Encyclopedia of **California Pottery**, Chipman	$24.95
4811	Collector's Encyclopedia of **Colorado Pottery**, Carlton	$24.95
2133	Collector's Encyclopedia of **Cookie Jars**, Roerig	$24.95
3723	Collector's Encyclopedia of **Cookie Jars**, Book II, Roerig	$24.95
4939	Collector's Encyclopedia of **Cookie Jars**, Book III, Roerig	$24.95
4638	Collector's Encyclopedia of **Dakota Potteries**, Dommel	$24.95
5040	Collector's Encyclopedia of **Fiesta**, 8th Ed., Huxford	$19.95
4718	Collector's Encyclopedia of **Figural Planters & Vases**, Newbound	$19.95
3961	Collector's Encyclopedia of **Early Noritake**, Alden	$24.95
1439	Collector's Encyclopedia of **Flow Blue China**, Gaston	$19.95
3812	Collector's Encyclopedia of **Flow Blue China**, 2nd Ed., Gaston	$24.95
3813	Collector's Encyclopedia of **Hall China**, 2nd Ed., Whitmyer	$24.95
1431	Collector's Encyclopedia of **Homer Laughlin China**, Jasper	$24.95
1276	Collector's Encyclopedia of **Hull Pottery**, Roberts	$19.95
3962	Collector's Encyclopedia of **Lefton China**, DeLozier	$19.95
4855	Collector's Encyclopedia of **Lefton China**, Book II, DeLozier	$19.95
2210	Collector's Encyclopedia of **Limoges Porcelain**, 2nd Ed., Gaston	$24.95
2334	Collector's Encyclopedia of **Majolica Pottery**, Katz-Marks	$19.95
1358	Collector's Encyclopedia of **McCoy Pottery**, Huxford	$19.95
3963	Collector's Encyclopedia of **Metlox Potteries**, Gibbs Jr.	$24.95
1837	Collector's Encyclopedia of **Nippon Porcelain**, Van Patten	$24.95
2089	Collector's Ency. of **Nippon Porcelain**, 2nd Series, Van Patten	$24.95
1665	Collector's Ency. of **Nippon Porcelain**, 3rd Series, Van Patten	$24.95
4712	Collector's Ency. of **Nippon Porcelain**, 4th Series, Van Patten	$24.95
1447	Collector's Encyclopedia of **Noritake**, Van Patten	$19.95
1432	Collector's Encyclopedia of **Noritake**, 2nd Series, Van Patten	$24.95
2037	Collector's Encyclopedia of **Occupied Japan**, 1st Series, Florence	$14.95
2038	Collector's Encyclopedia of **Occupied Japan**, 2nd Series, Florence	$14.95
2088	Collector's Encyclopedia of **Occupied Japan**, 3rd Series, Florence	$14.95
2019	Collector's Encyclopedia of **Occupied Japan**, 4th Series, Florence	$14.95
2335	Collector's Encyclopedia of **Occupied Japan**, 5th Series, Florence	$14.95
1951	Collector's Encyclopedia of **Old Ivory China**, Hillman	$24.95
3964	Collector's Encyclopedia of **Pickard China**, Reed	$24.95
1877	Collector's Encyclopedia of **R.S. Prussia**, 4th Series, Gaston	$24.95
4034	Collector's Encyclopedia of **Roseville Pottery**, Huxford	$19.95
4035	Collector's Encyclopedia of **Roseville Pottery**, 2nd Ed., Huxford	$19.95
1856	Collector's Encyclopeida of **Russel Wright**, 2nd Ed., Kerr	$24.95
2713	Collector's Encyclopedia of **Salt Glaze Stoneware**, Taylor/Lowrance	$24.95
3314	Collector's Encyclopedia of **Van Briggle** Art Pottery, Sasicki	$24.95
1563	Collector's Encyclopedia of **Wall Pockets**, Newbound	$19.95
3111	Collector's Encyclopedia of **Weller Pottery**, Huxford	$29.95
3876	Collector's Guide to **Lu-Ray Pastels**, Meehan	$18.95
3814	Collector's Guide to **Made in Japan** Ceramics, White	$18.95
4646	Collector's Guide to **Made in Japan** Ceramics, Book II, White	$18.95
4565	Collector's Guide to **Rockington**, The Enduring Ware, Brewer	$14.95
2339	Collector's Guide to **Shawnee Pottery**, Vanderbilt	$24.95
1425	**Cookie Jars**, Westfall	$9.95

3440	**Cookie Jars**, Book II, Westfall	$19.95
4924	Figural & Novelty **Salt & Pepper Shakers**, 2nd Series, Davern	$24.95
2379	Lehner's Ency. of **U.S. Marks** on Pottery, Porcelain & China	$24.95
4722	**McCoy Pottery**, Collector's Reference & Value Guide, Hanson/Nissen	$19.95
3825	**Purinton Pottery**, Morris	$24.95
4726	**Red Wing Art Pottery**, 1920s–1960s, Dollen	$19.95
1670	**Red Wing Collectibles**, DePasquale	$9.95
1440	**Red Wing Stoneware**, DePasquale	$9.95
1632	**Salt & Pepper Shakers**, Guarnaccia	$9.95
5091	**Salt & Pepper Shakers** II, Guarnaccia	$18.95
2220	**Salt & Pepper Shakers** III, Guarnaccia	$14.95
3443	**Salt & Pepper Shakers** IV, Guarnaccia	$18.95
3738	**Shawnee Pottery**, Mangus	$24.95
4629	Turn of the Century **American Dinnerware**, 1880s–1920s, Jasper	$24.95
4572	**Wall Pockets** of the Past, Perkins	$17.95
3327	**Watt Pottery** – Identification & Value Guide, Morris	$19.95

OTHER COLLECTIBLES

4704	Antique & Collectible **Buttons**, Wisniewski	$19.95
2269	Antique **Brass & Copper** Collectibles, Gaston	$16.95
1880	Antique **Iron**, McNerney	$9.95
3872	Antique **Tins**, Dodge	$24.95
4845	Antique **Typewriters & Office Collectibles**, Rehr	$19.95
1714	**Black** Collectibles, Gibbs	$19.95
1128	**Bottle** Pricing Guide, 3rd Ed., Cleveland	$7.95
4636	**Celluloid Collectibles**, Dunn	$14.95
3718	Collectible **Aluminum**, Grist	$16.95
3445	Collectible **Cats**, An Identification & Value Guide, Fyke	$18.95
4560	Collectible **Cats**, An Identification & Value Guide, Book II, Fyke	$19.95
4852	Collectible **Compact Disc** Price Guide 2, Cooper	$17.95
2018	Collector's Encyclopedia of **Granite Ware**, Greguire	$24.95
3430	Collector's Encyclopedia of **Granite Ware**, Book 2, Greguire	$24.95
4705	Collector's Guide to **Antique Radios**, 4th Ed., Bunis	$18.95
3880	Collector's Guide to **Cigarette Lighters**, Flanagan	$17.95
4637	Collector's Guide to **Cigarette Lighers**, Book II, Flanagan	$17.95
4942	Collector's Guide to **Don Winton Designs**, Ellis	$19.95
3966	Collector's Guide to **Inkwells**, Identification & Values, Badders	$18.95
4947	Collector's Guide to **Inkwells**, Book II, Badders	$19.95
4948	Collector's Guide to **Letter Openers**, Grist	$19.95
4862	Collector's Guide to **Toasters** & Accessories, Greguire	$19.95
4652	Collector's Guide to **Transistor Radios**, 2nd Ed., Bunis	$16.95
4653	Collector's Guide to **TV Memorabilia**, 1960s–1970s, Davis/Morgan	$24.95
4864	Collector's Guide to **Wallace Nutting Pictures**, Ivankovich	$18.95
1629	**Doorstops**, Identification & Values, Bertoia	$9.95
4567	Figural **Napkin Rings**, Gottschalk & Whitson	$18.95
4717	Figural **Nodders**, Includes Bobbin' Heads and Swayers, Irtz	$19.95
3968	**Fishing Lure** Collectibles, Murphy/Edmisten	$24.95
4867	**Flea Market Trader**, 11th Ed., Huxford	$9.95
4944	**Flue Covers**, Collector's Value Guide, Meckley	$12.95
4945	**G-Men and FBI Toys** and Collectibles, Whitworth	$18.95
5043	**Garage Sale & Flea Market Annual**, 6th Ed.	$19.95
3819	**General Store Collectibles**, Wilson	$24.95
4643	**Great American West** Collectibles, Wilson	$24.95
2215	Goldstein's **Coca-Cola** Collectibles	$16.95
3884	Huxford's **Collectible Advertising**, 2nd Ed.	$24.95
2216	**Kitchen Antiques**, 1790–1940, McNerney	$14.95
4950	The **Lone Ranger**, Collector's Reference & Value Guide, Felbinger	$18.95
2026	**Railroad** Collectibles, 4th Ed., Baker	$14.95
4949	**Schroeder's Antiques Price Guide**, 16th Ed., Huxford	$12.95
5007	**Silverplated Flatware**, Revised 4th Edition, Hagan	$18.95
1922	Standard **Old Bottle** Price Guide, Sellari	$14.95
4708	Summers' Guide to **Coca-Cola**	$19.95
4952	Summers' Pocket Guide to **Coca-Cola** Identifications	$9.95
3892	**Toy & Miniature Sewing Machines**, Thomas	$18.95
4876	**Toy & Miniature Sewing Machines**, Book II, Thomas	$24.95
3828	Value Guide to **Advertising Memorabilia**, Summers	$18.95
3977	Value Guide to **Gas Station** Memorabilia, Summers & Priddy	$24.95
4877	Vintage **Bar Ware**, Visakay	$24.95
4935	The W.F. Cody **Buffalo Bill** Collector's Guide with Values	$24.95
4879	**Wanted to Buy**, 6th Edition	$9.95

Schroeder's
ANTIQUES
Price Guide

. . . is the #1 best-selling antiques & collectibles value guide on the market today, and here's why . . .

![Schroeder's Antiques Price Guide book cover]
Schroeder's
ANTIQUES
Price Guide

OUR #1 BEST SELLER!

Identification & Values Of Over 50,000 Antiques & Collectibles

8½ x 11, 608 Pages, $12.95

• *More than 300 advisors, well-known dealers, and top-notch collectors work together with our editors to bring you accurate information regarding pricing and identification.*

• *More than 45,000 items in almost 500 categories are listed along with hundreds of sharp original photos that illustrate not only the rare and unusual, but the common, popular collectibles as well.*

• *Each large close-up shot shows important details clearly. Every subject is represented with histories and background information, a feature not found in any of our competitors' publications.*

• *Our editors keep abreast of newly developing trends, often adding several new categories a year as the need arises.*

If it merits the interest of today's collector, you'll find it in *Schroeder's*. And you can feel confident that the information we publish is up to date and accurate. Our advisors thoroughly check each category to spot inconsistencies, listings that may not be entirely reflective of market dealings, and lines too vague to be of merit. Only the best of the lot remains for publication.

Without doubt, you'll find
SCHROEDER'S ANTIQUES PRICE GUIDE
the only one to buy for
reliable information and values.

COLLECTOR BOOKS
A Division of Schroeder Publishing Co., Inc.